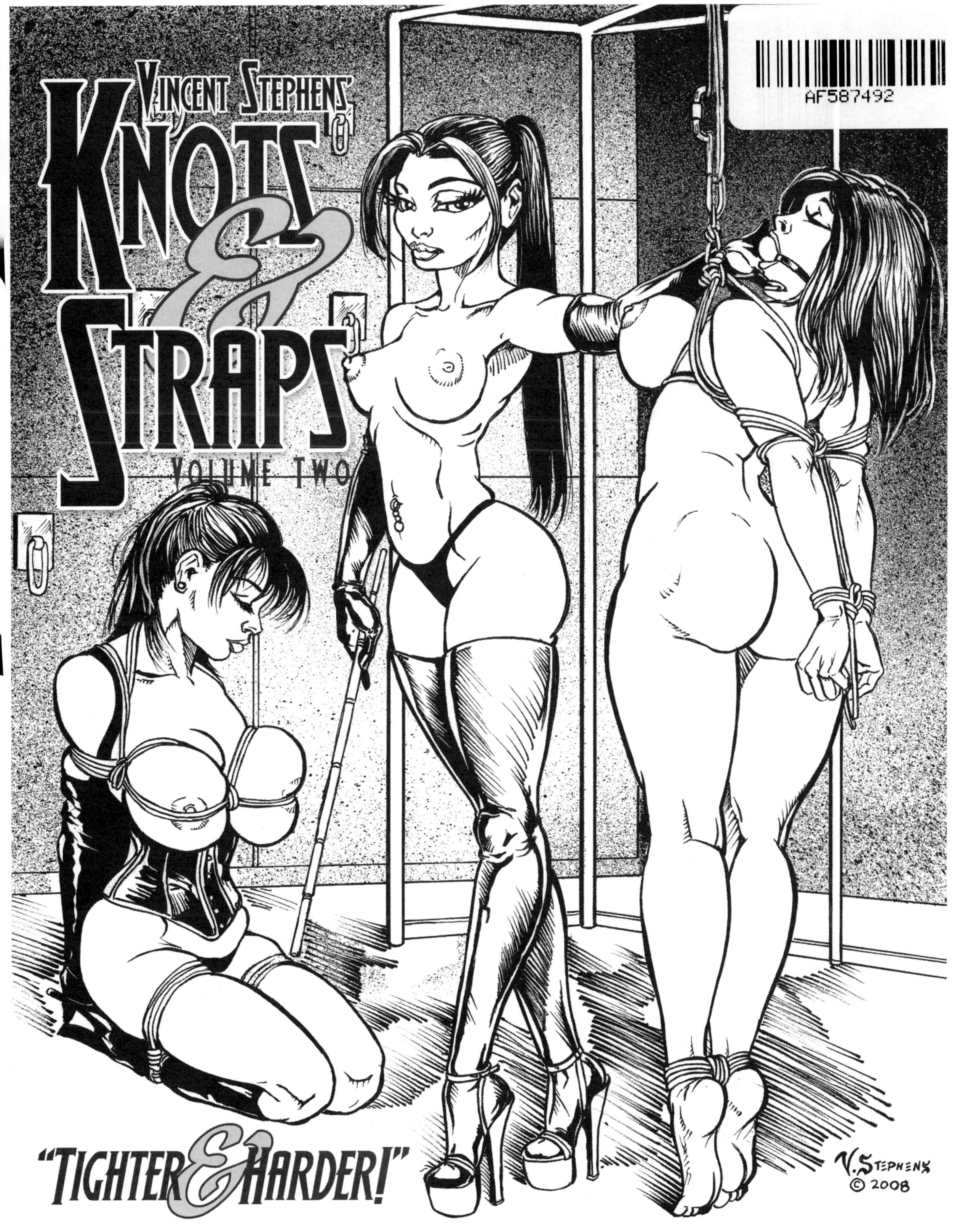

AN SQP PRESENTATION

Vincent Stephens 2 - Tighter & Wiser!

Artist and provocateur of all things pretty, pierced, tattooed or tied up - speaks!

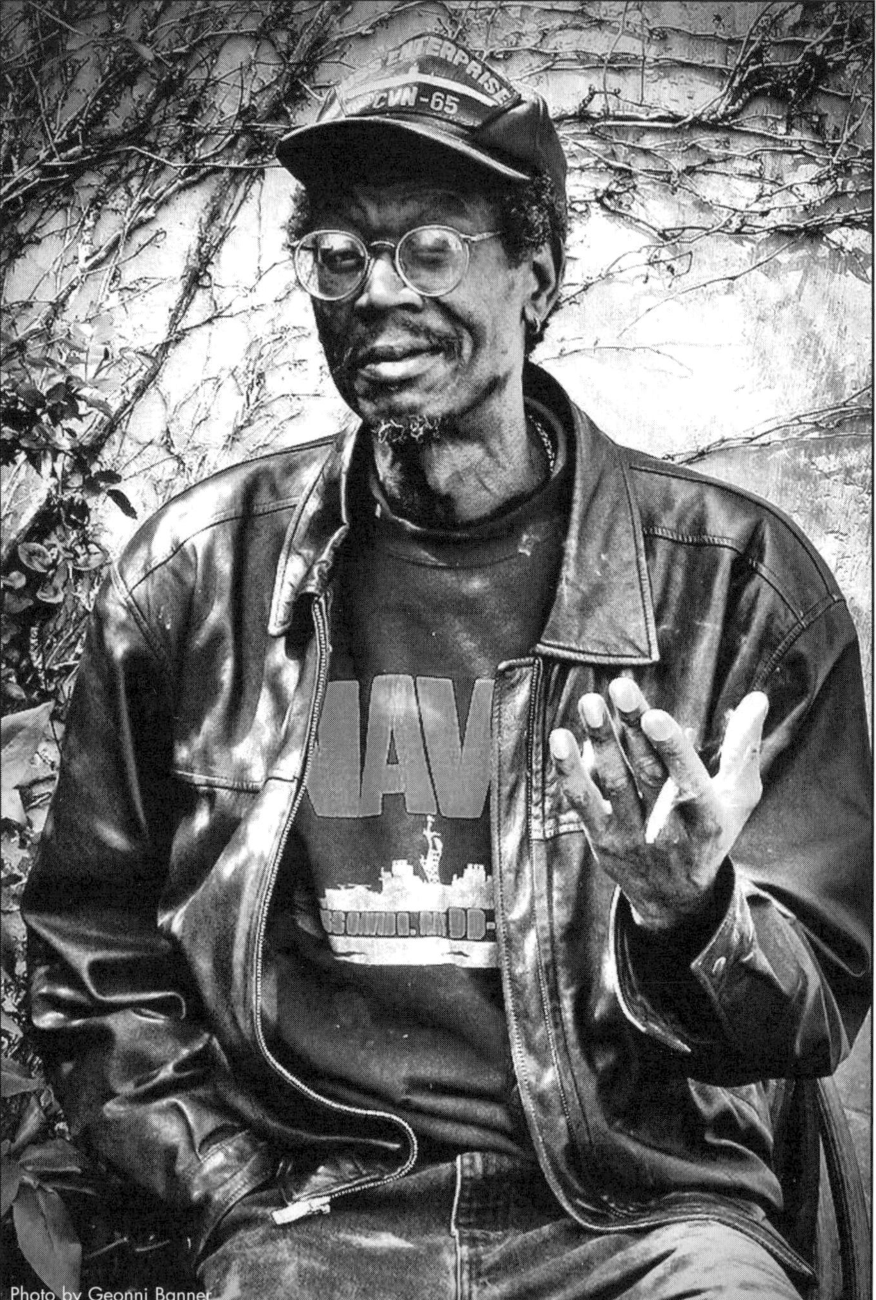

Photo by Geonni Banner

First and foremost I'd like to state how gratified I am that volume one of ***Knots & Straps*** was so well received by fans and supporters. For that I would like to extend thanks to all of you who continue to follow my work.

So here we are again with another presentation of various and sundry bits of fun that, by and large, I've created since the last time around. Now, I realize that there may be some who might say "*Hey! There's not enough knots!*" or "*I wanted more straps*". The truth is that this is a collection of pieces that covers a range of things from cute/edgy/toony to..um...not-so-toony, but all more or less falling under the big tent of fetish-y bondage-y tatted pierced lingerie'd (or outright nude) pinup sexiness. It's my hope that you'll enjoy them.

For those who would like to see what other shenanigans I might be perpetrating, please feel free to swing by my website. I had recently shifted to a new domain, so those of you who'd thought I'd dropped of the face of the earth can find my web presence at ***www.ramstarart.com***.

Again, I must give my heartfelt thanks to Mark McNabb for the kickass color on the cover, the good folks at SQP for this opportunity to put this work before you, and, of course, to you for picking it up.

Stay tuned. There's bound to be more fun in the times ahead.

Vincent Stephens

Vincent Stephens'

KNOTS & STRAPS

Volume Two

Book design by Grassy Knoll Studios.
Publishers: Sal Quartuccio and Bob Keenan

Published by
SQP Inc.
PO Box 248 - Columbus, NJ 08022

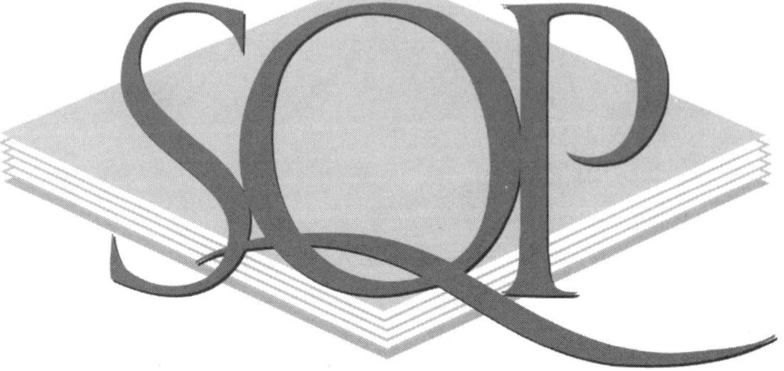

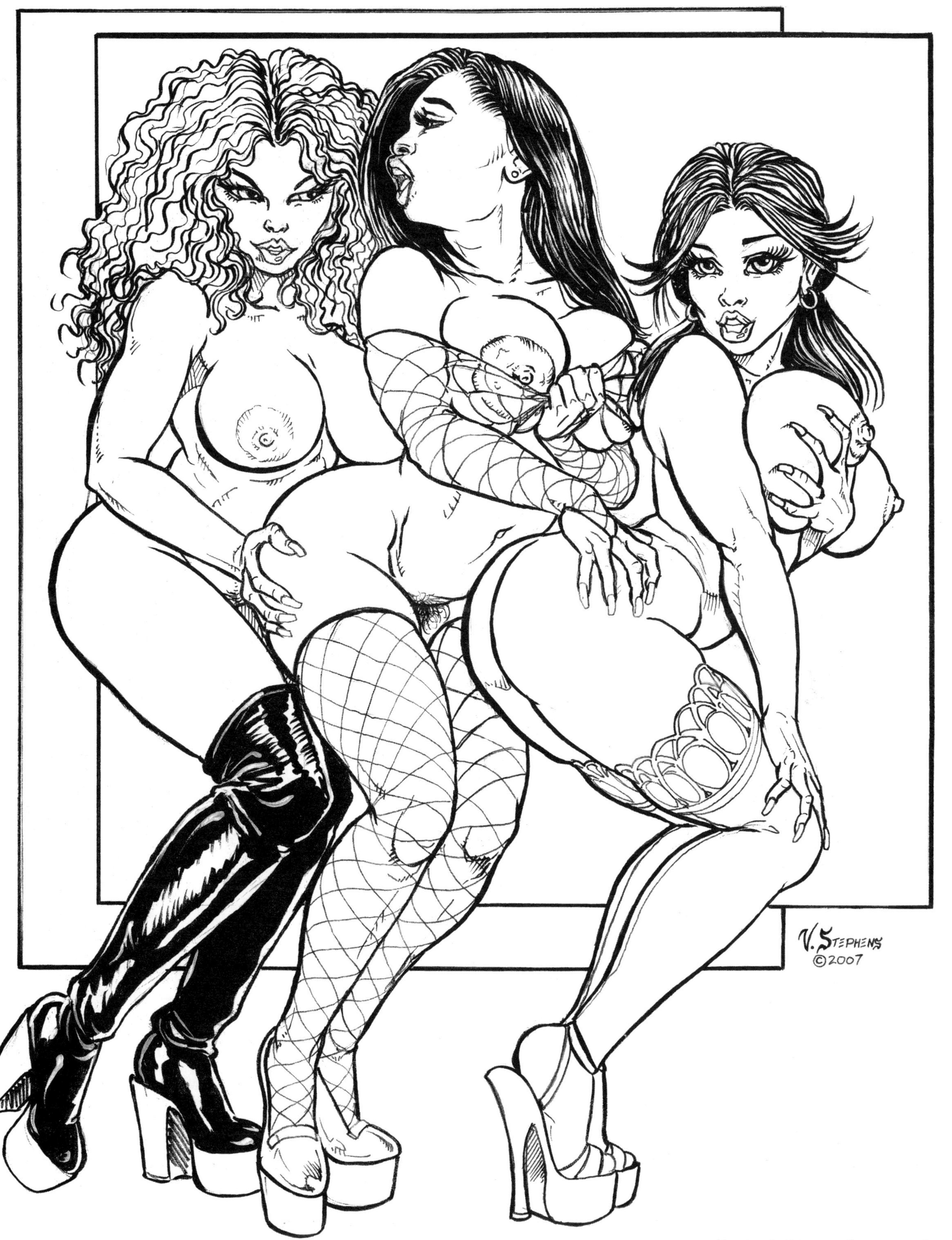
V. Stephens
©2007

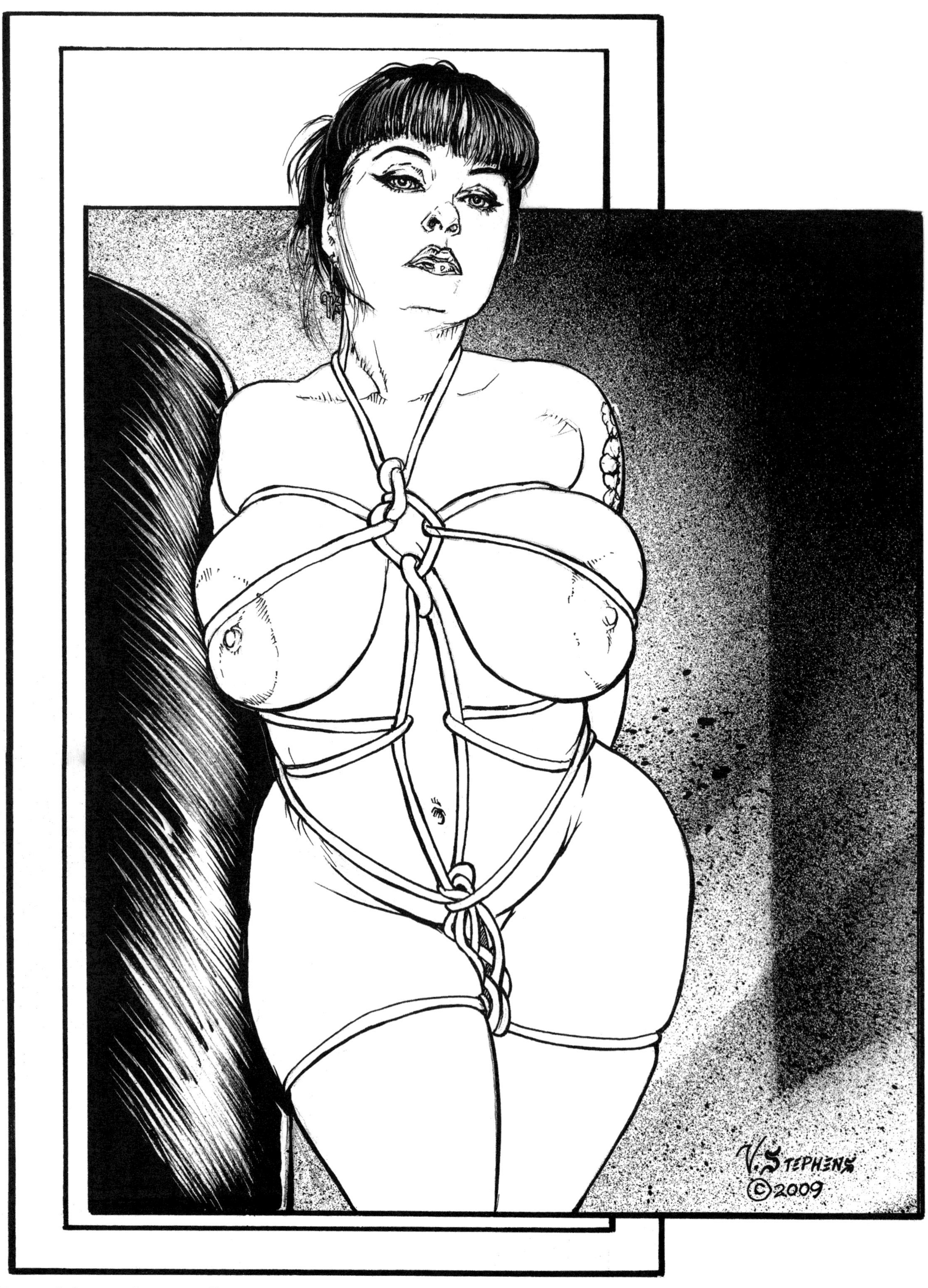
V. STEPHENS
©2009

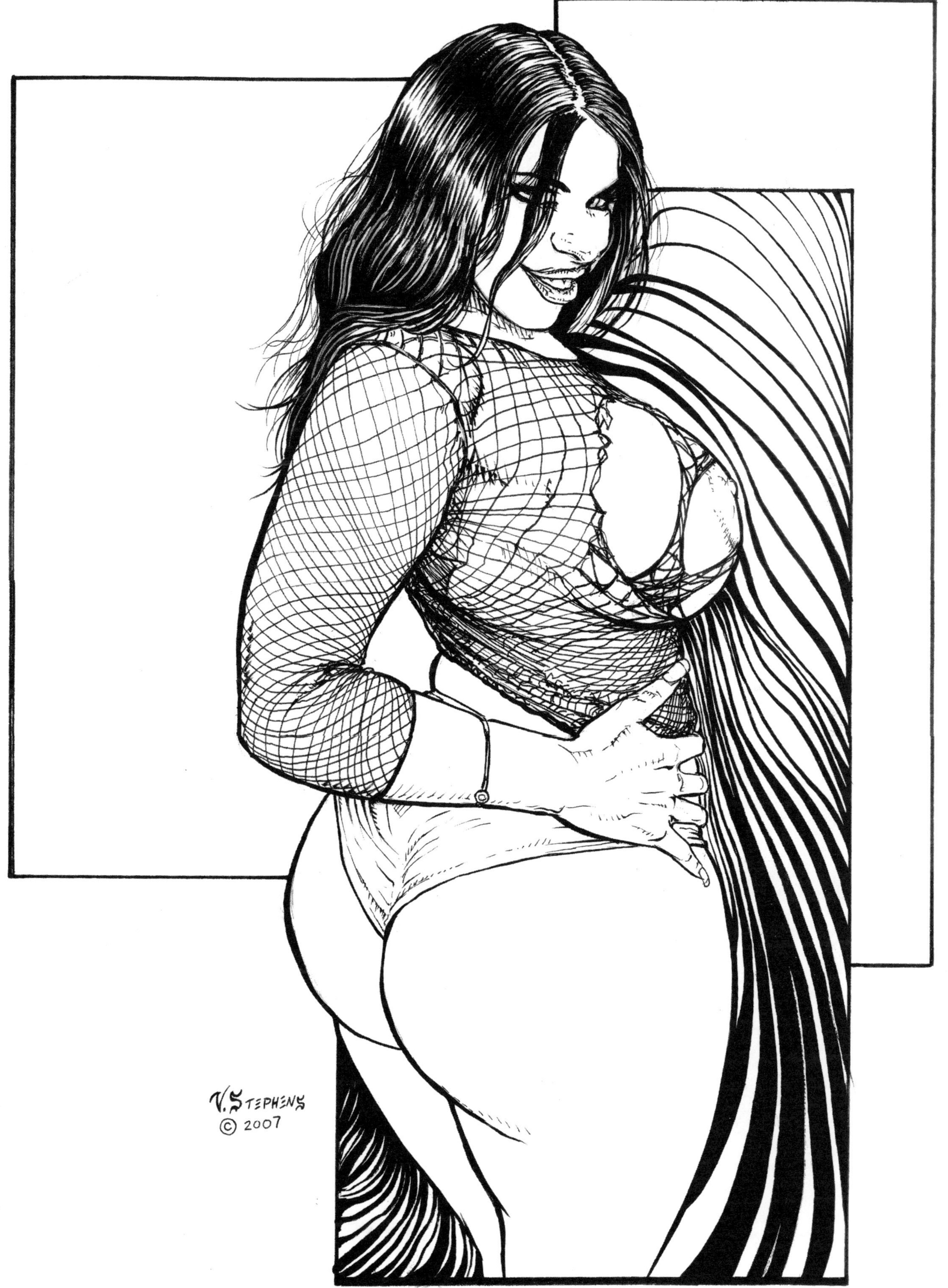
V. Stephens
© 2007

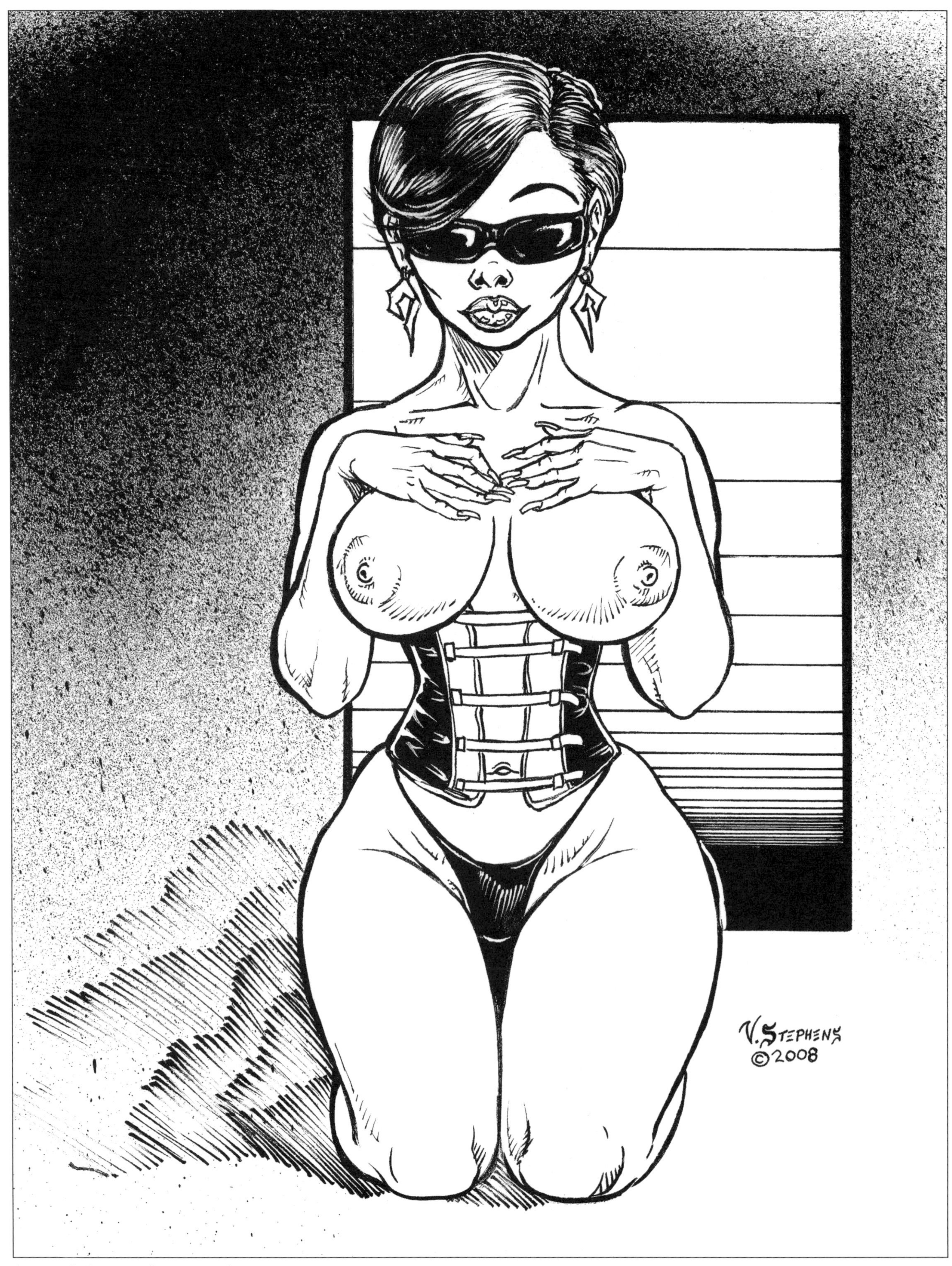
V. STEPHENS
©2008

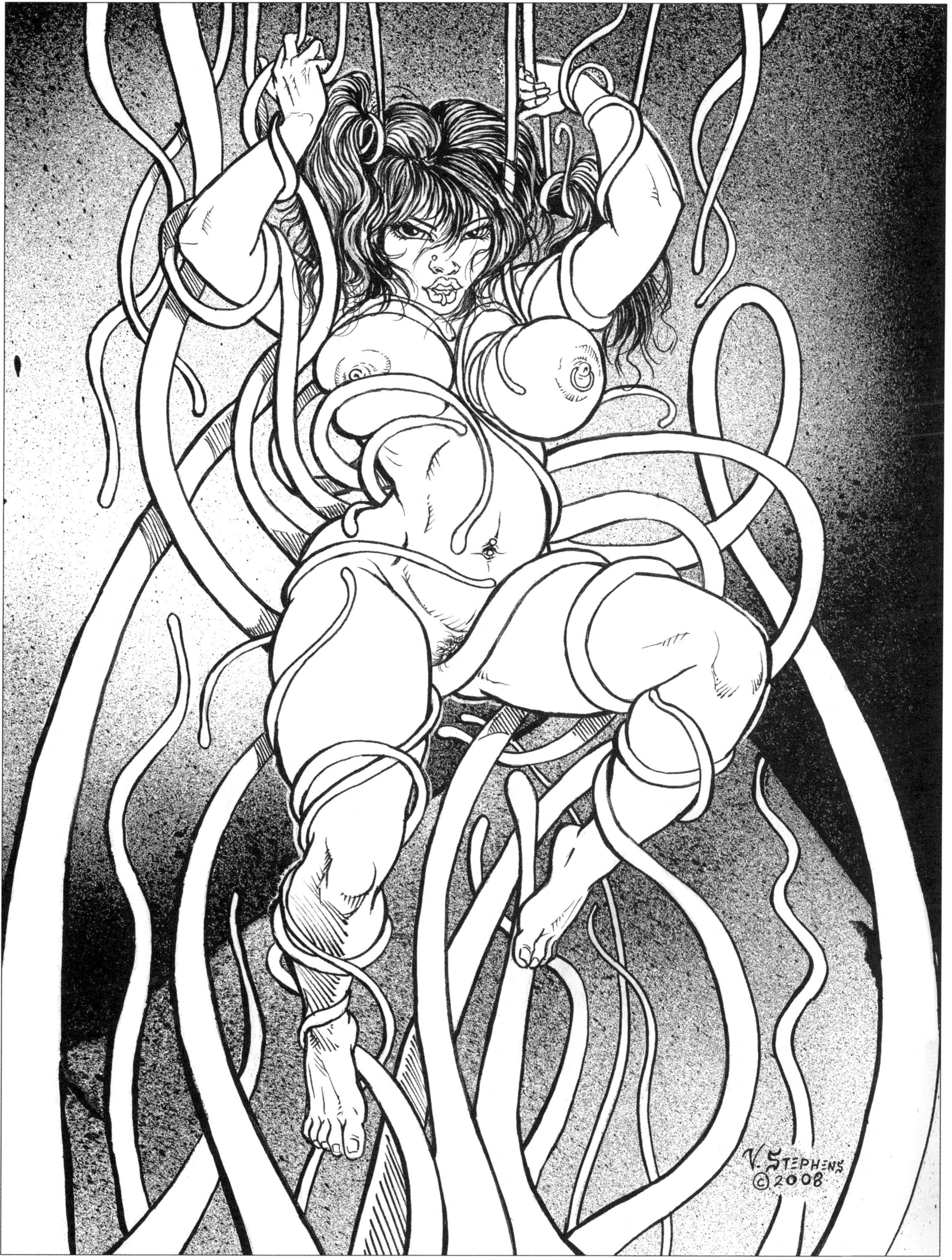
V. STEPHENS
©2008

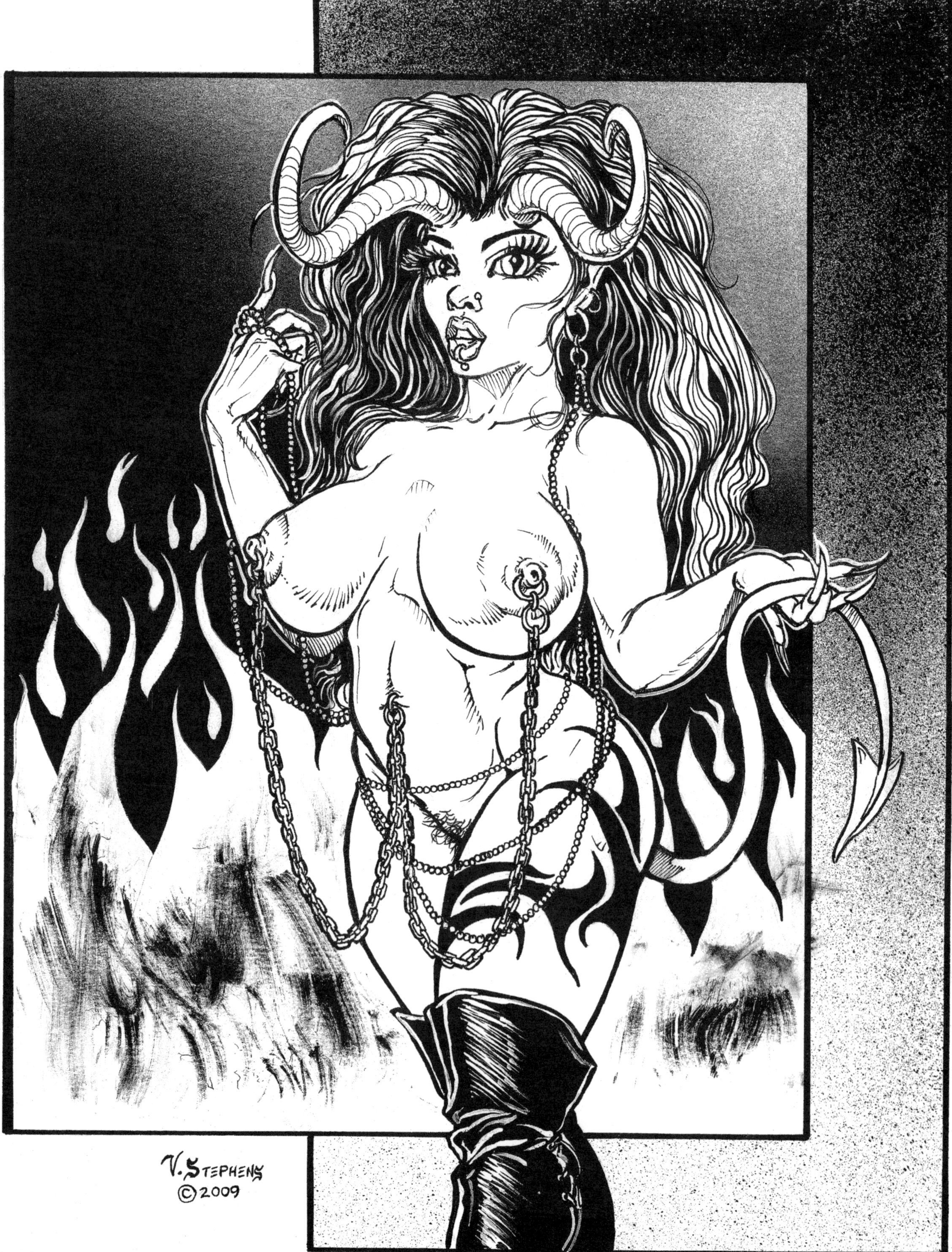
V. STEPHENS
©2009

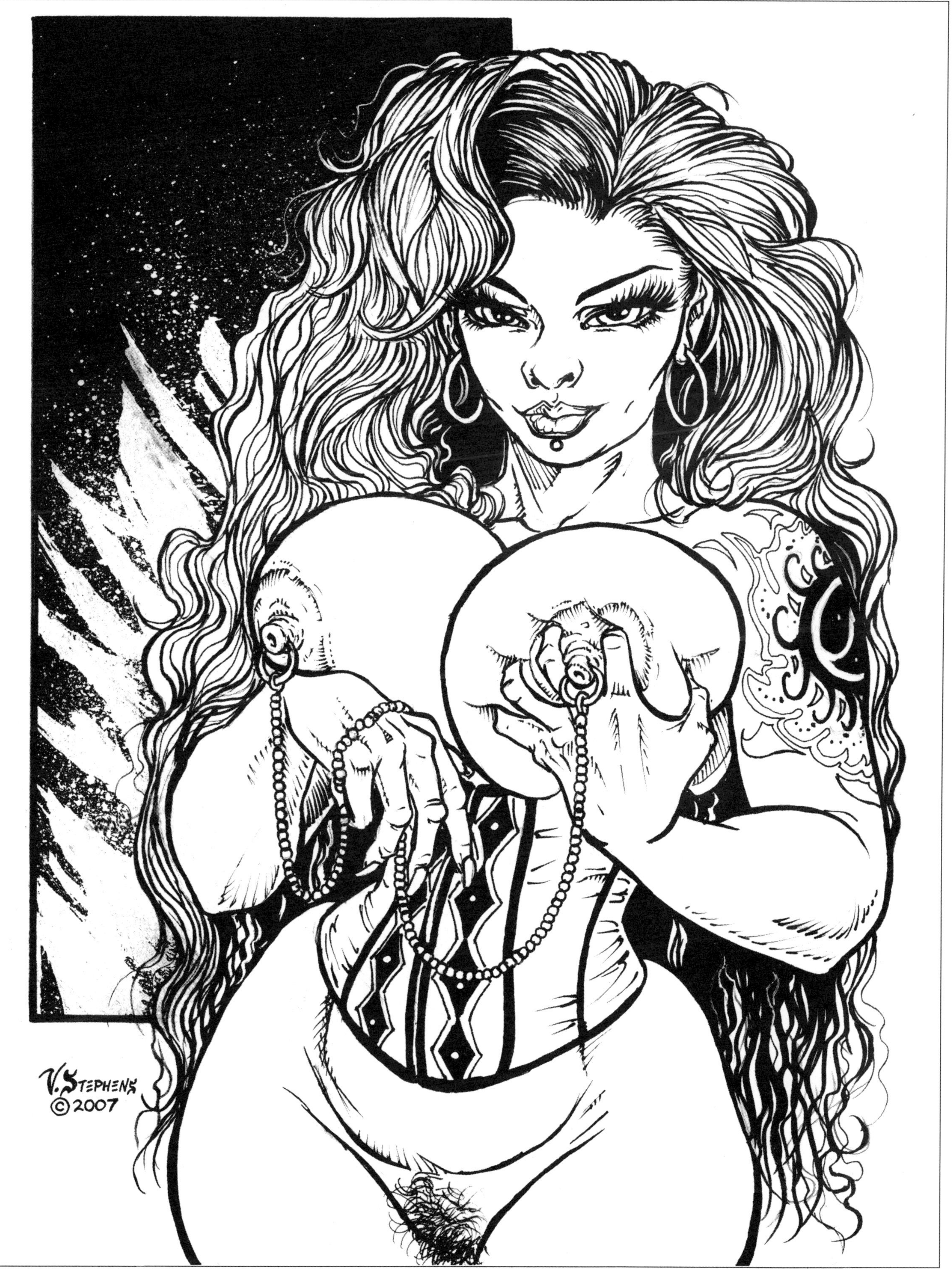
V.STEPHENS
©2007

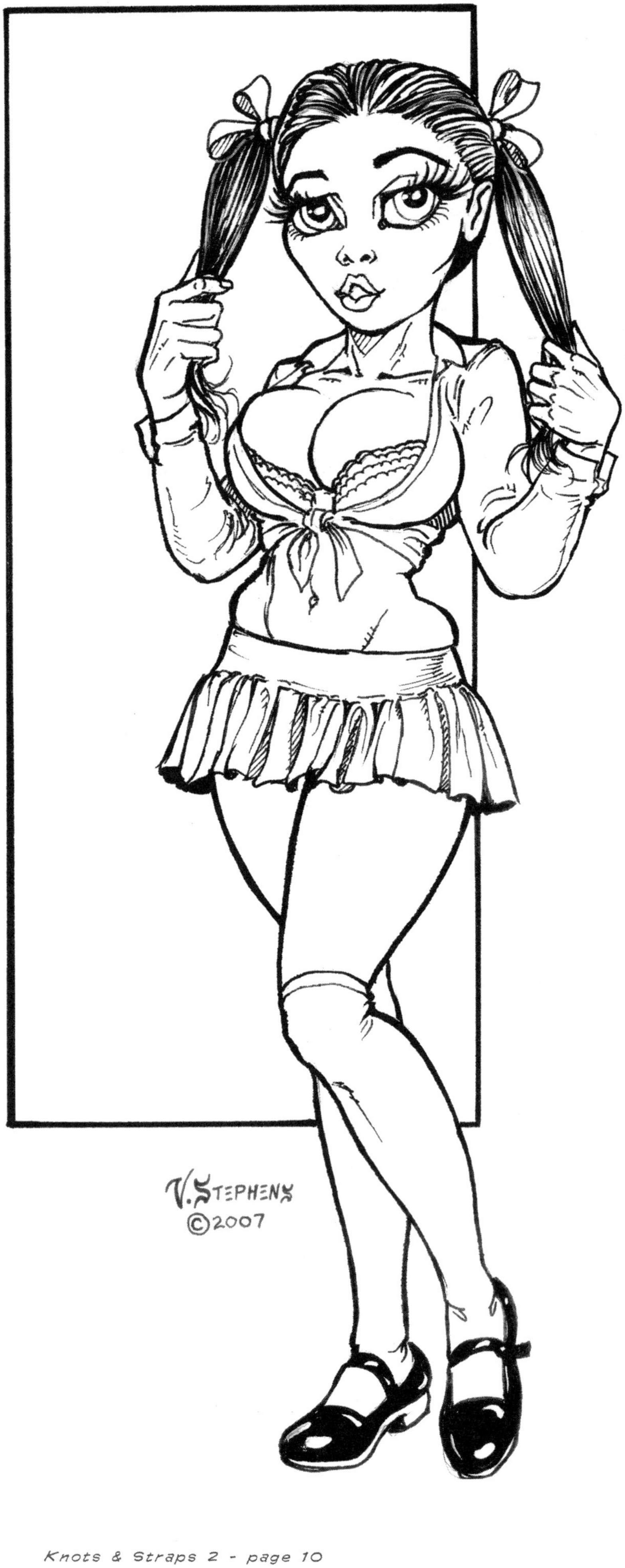

V.Stephens
©2007

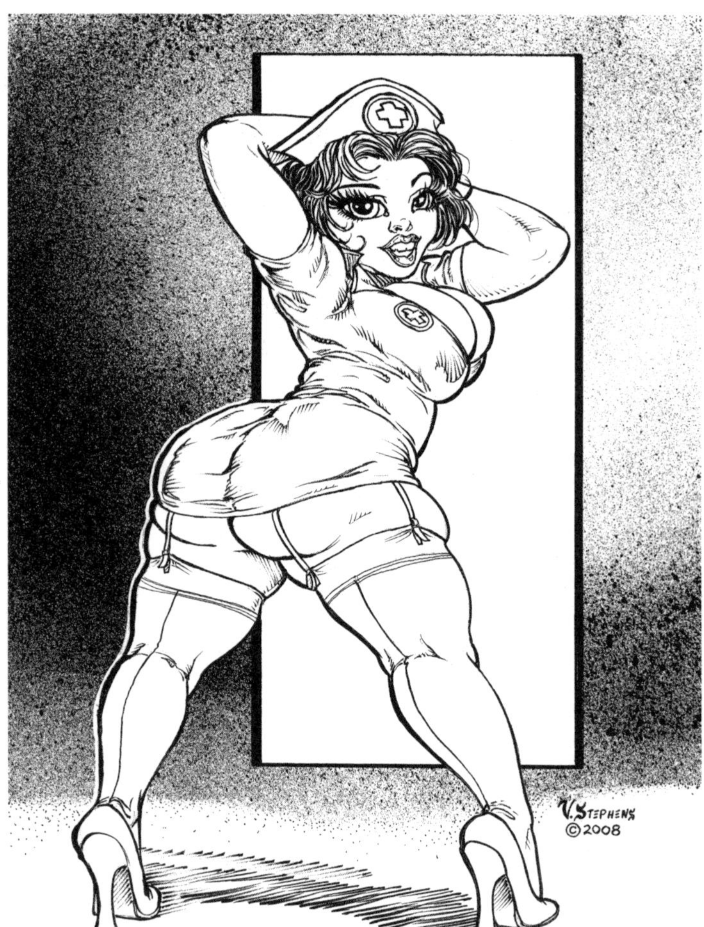

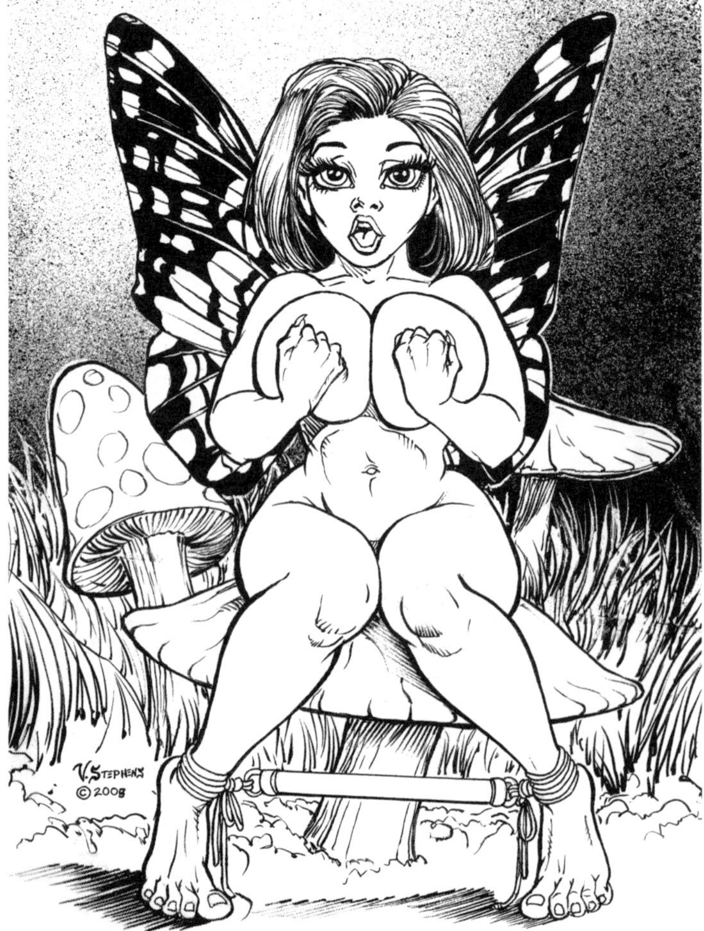

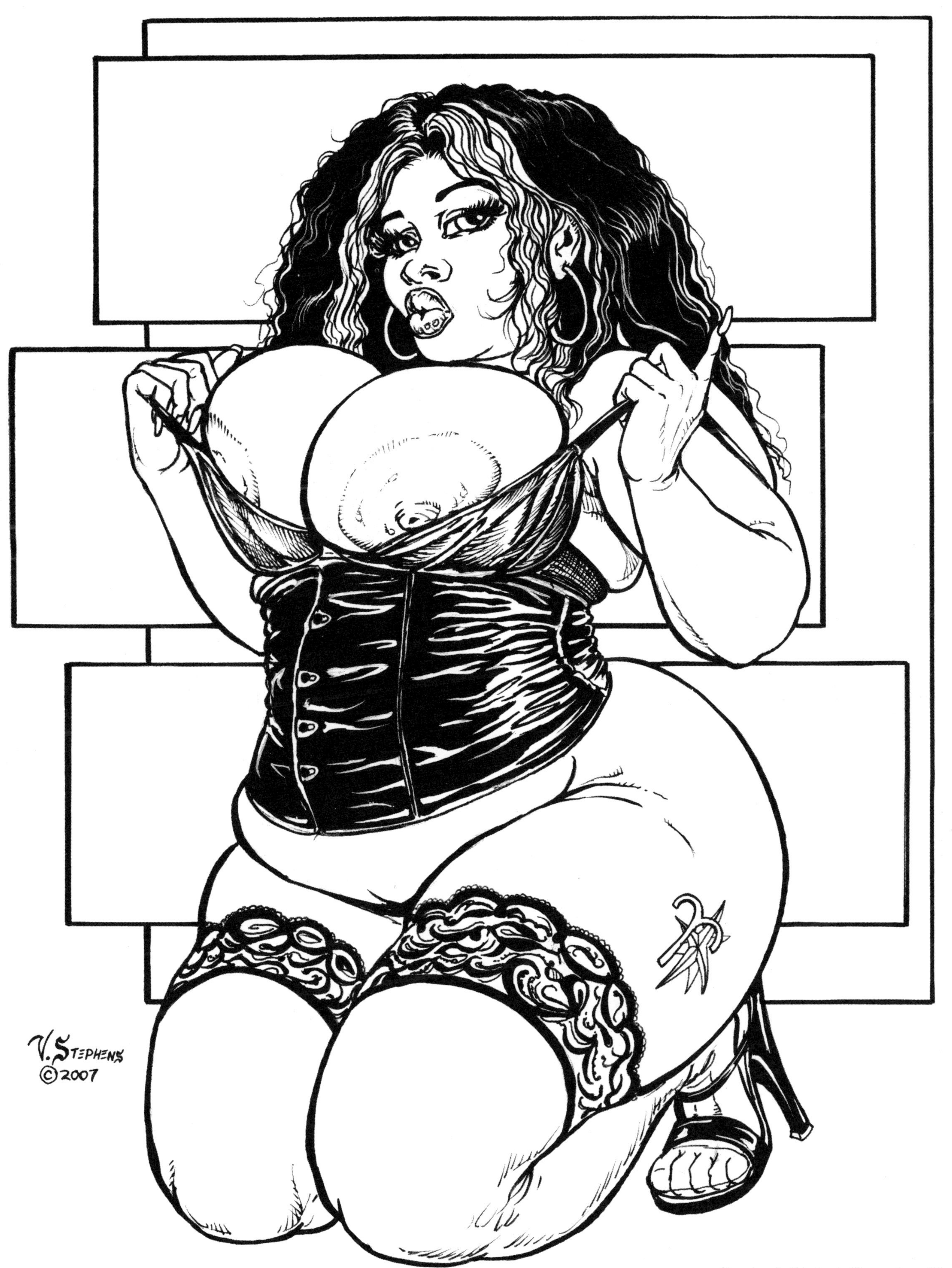
V. Stephens
©2007

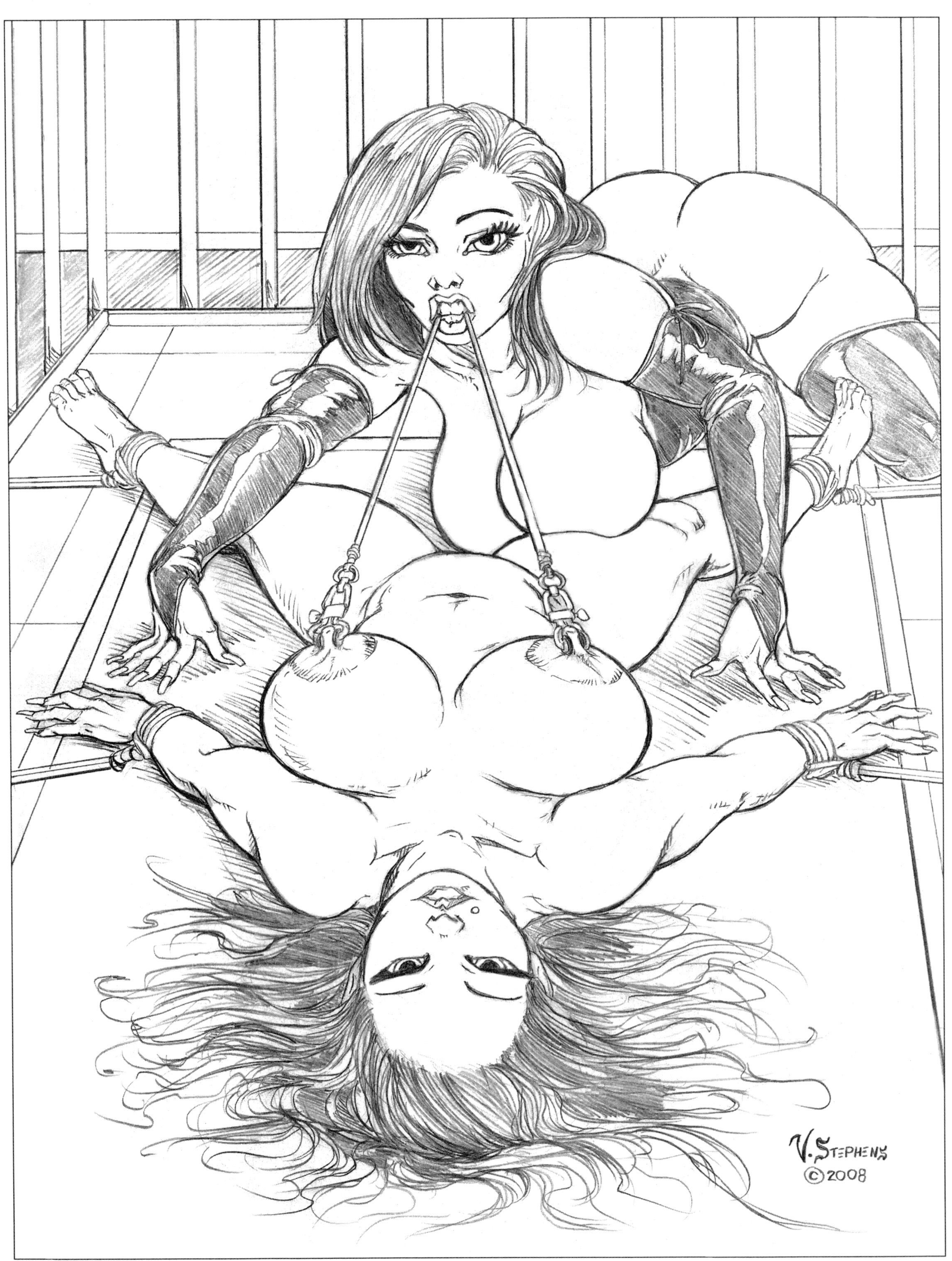
V. Stephens
©2008

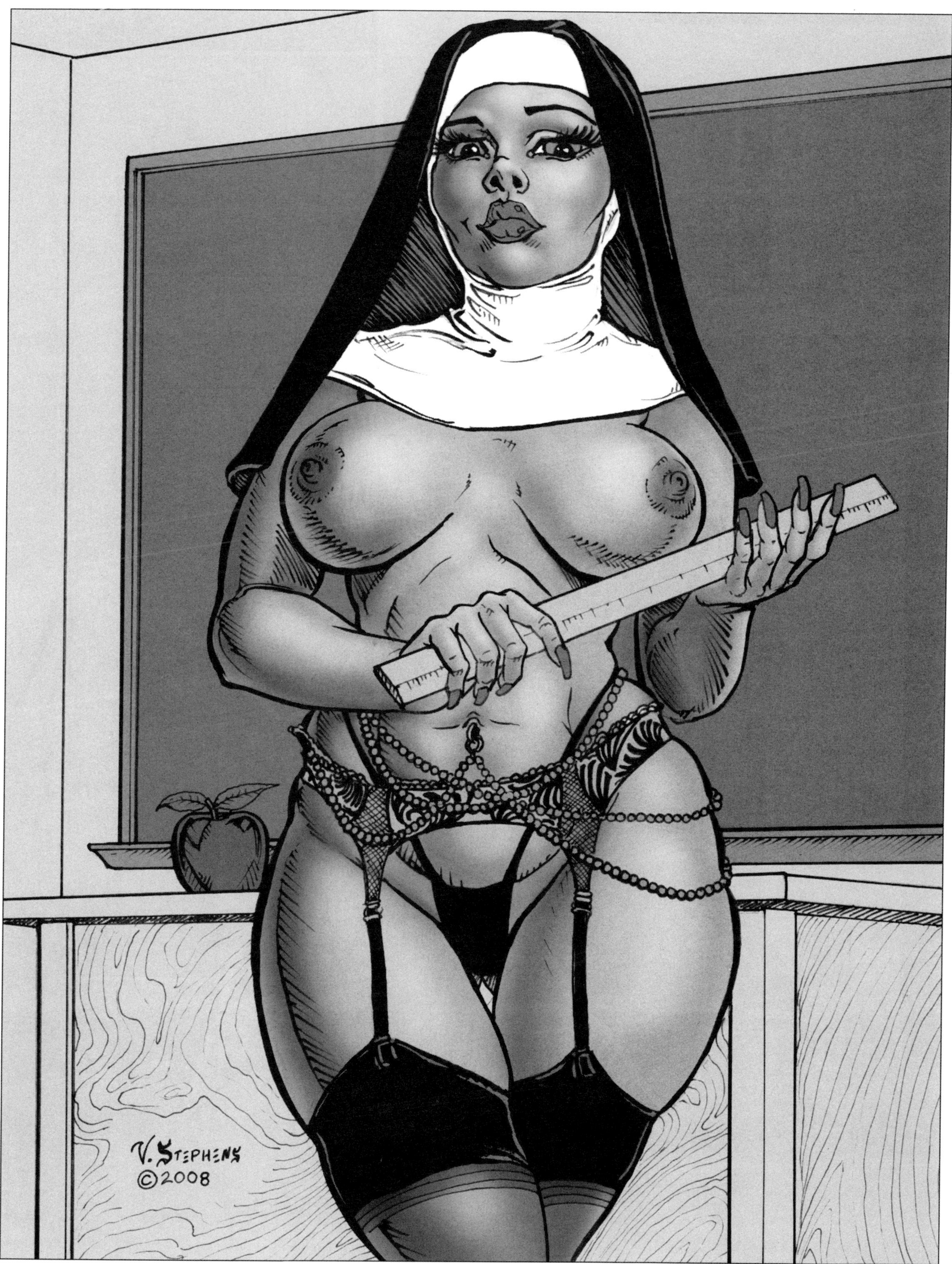
V. STEPHENS
©2008

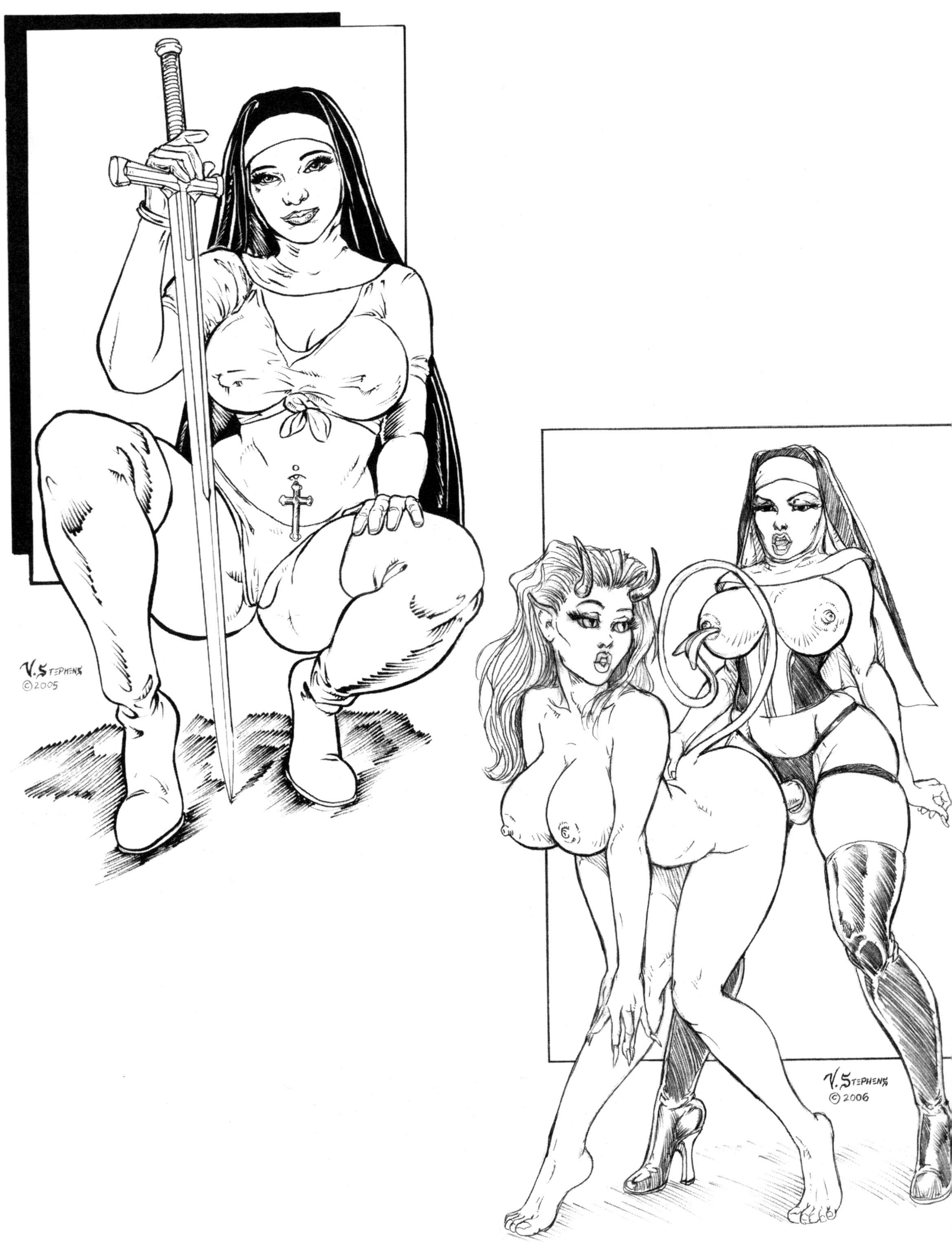
V. Stephens
©2005
V. Stephens
©2006

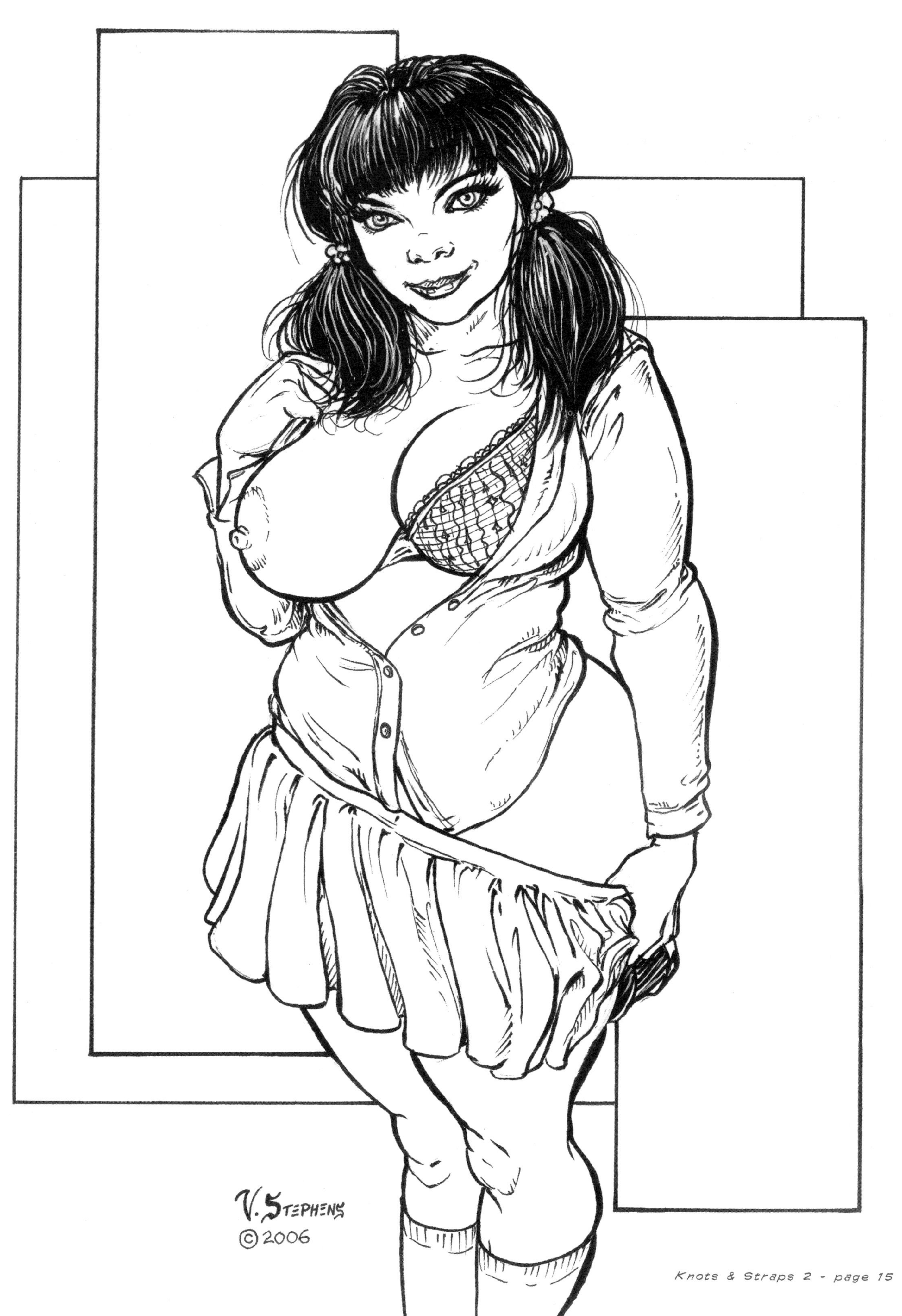
V. Stephens
©2006

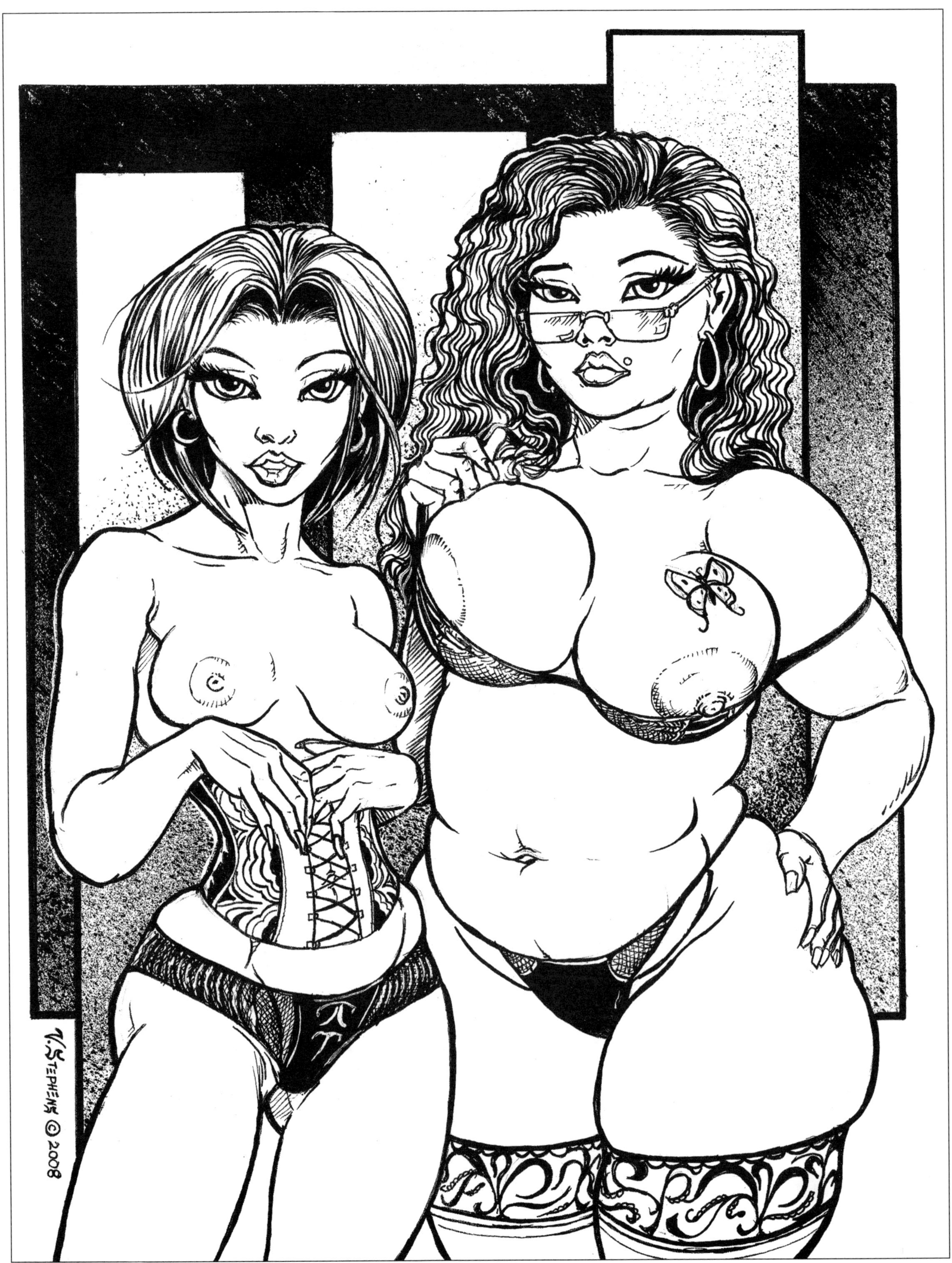
V.Stephens © 2008

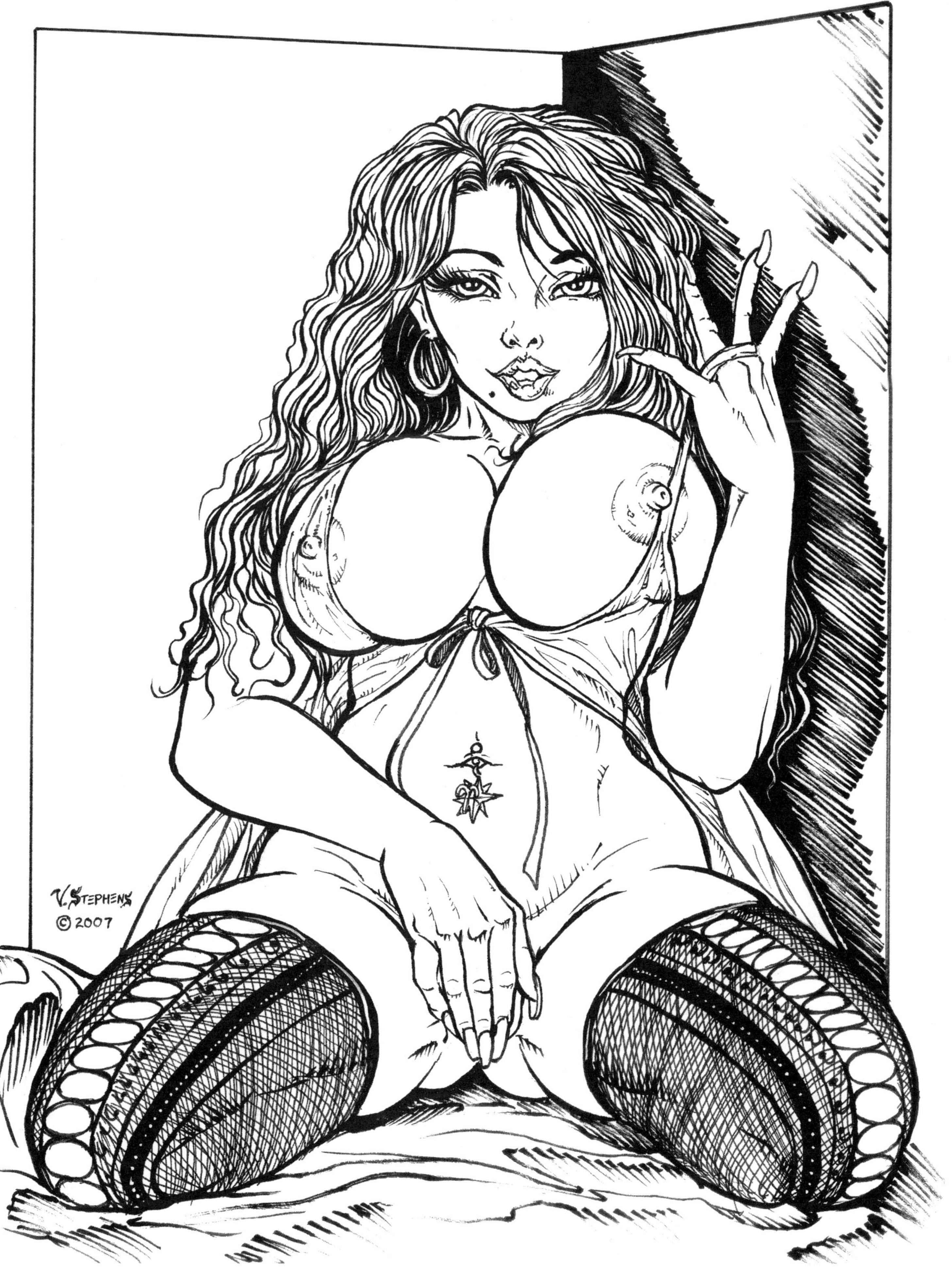
V. STEPHENS
© 2007

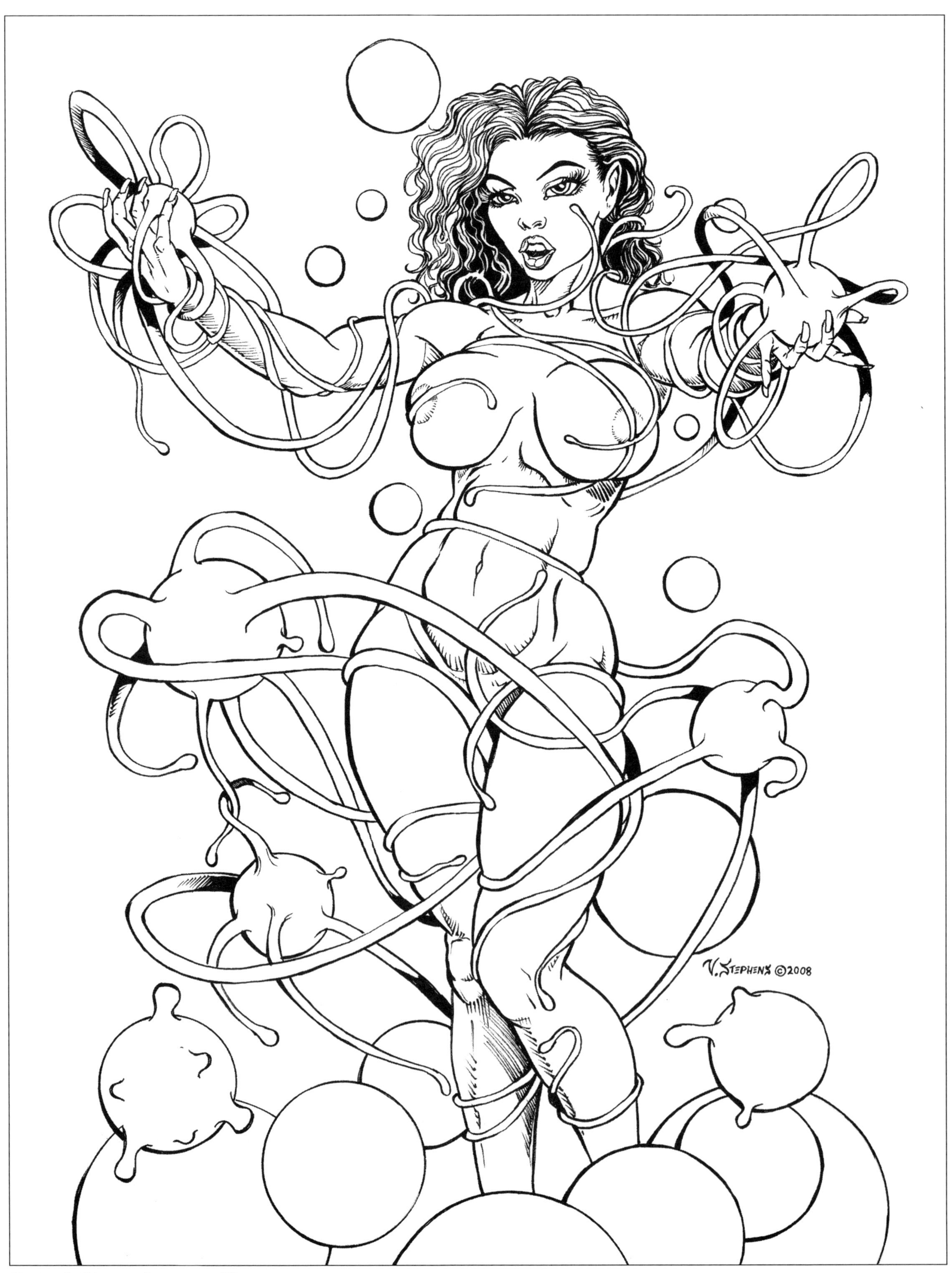
V. Stephens ©2008

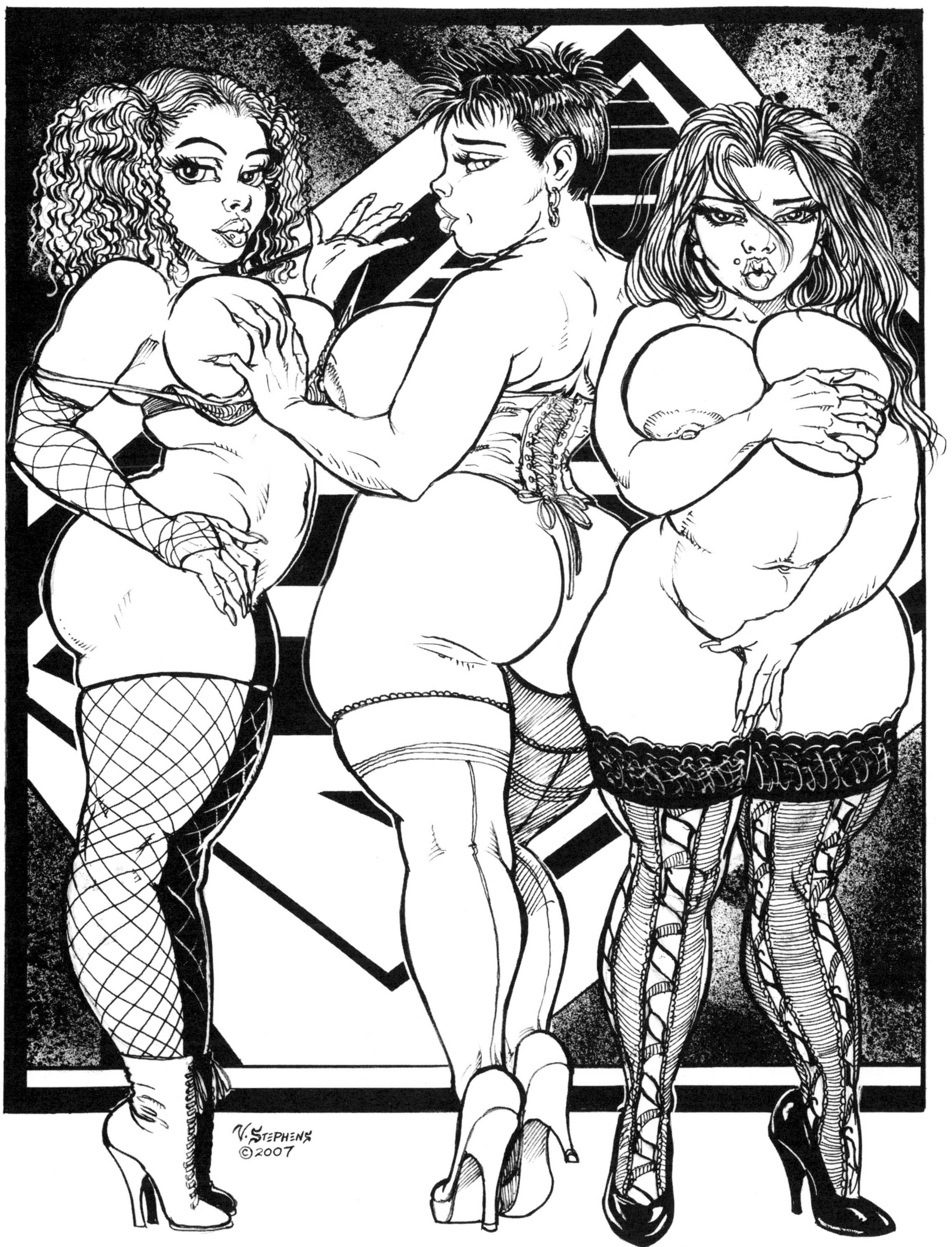
V. STEPHENS
©2007

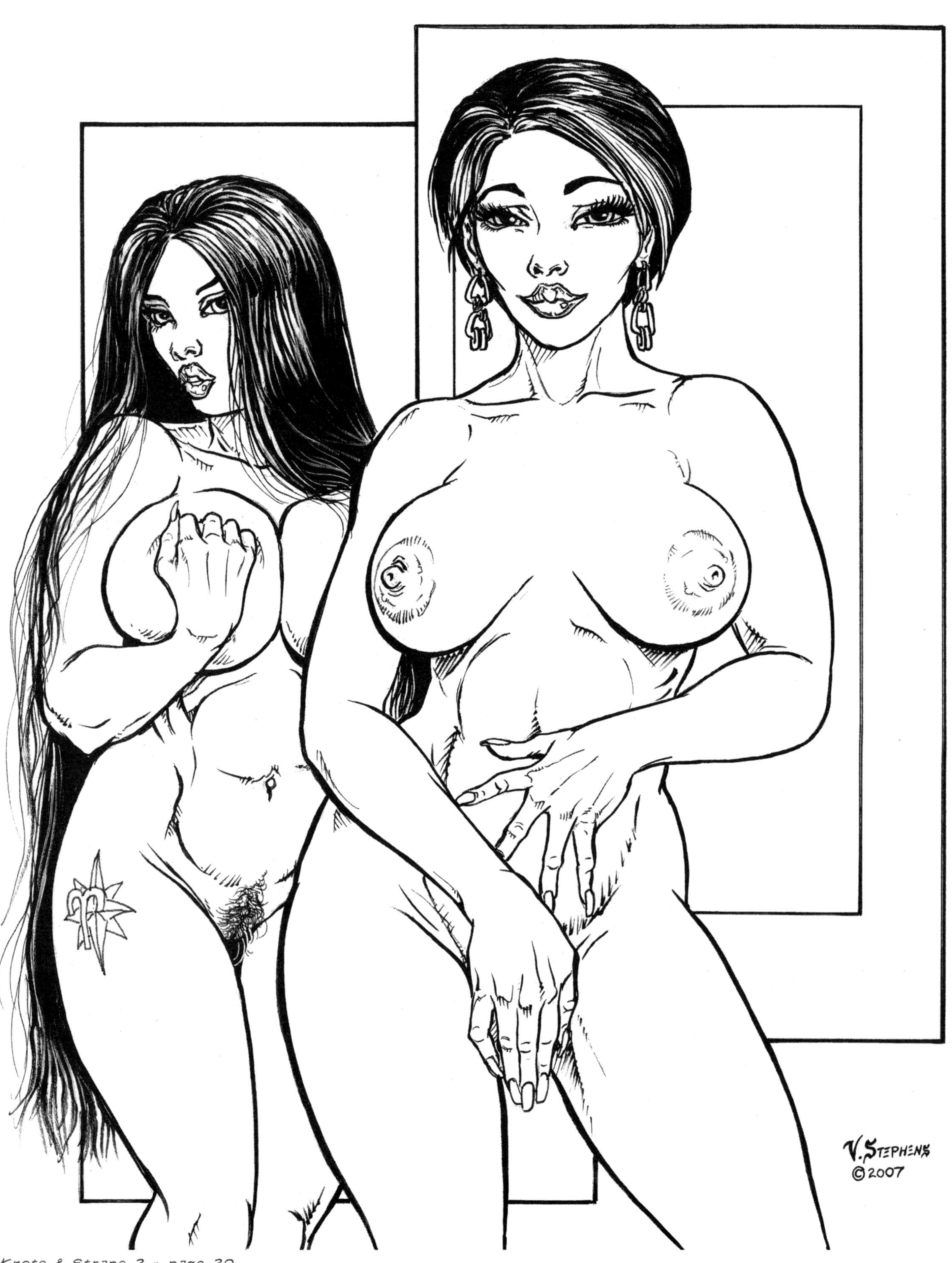
V. STEPHENS
©2007

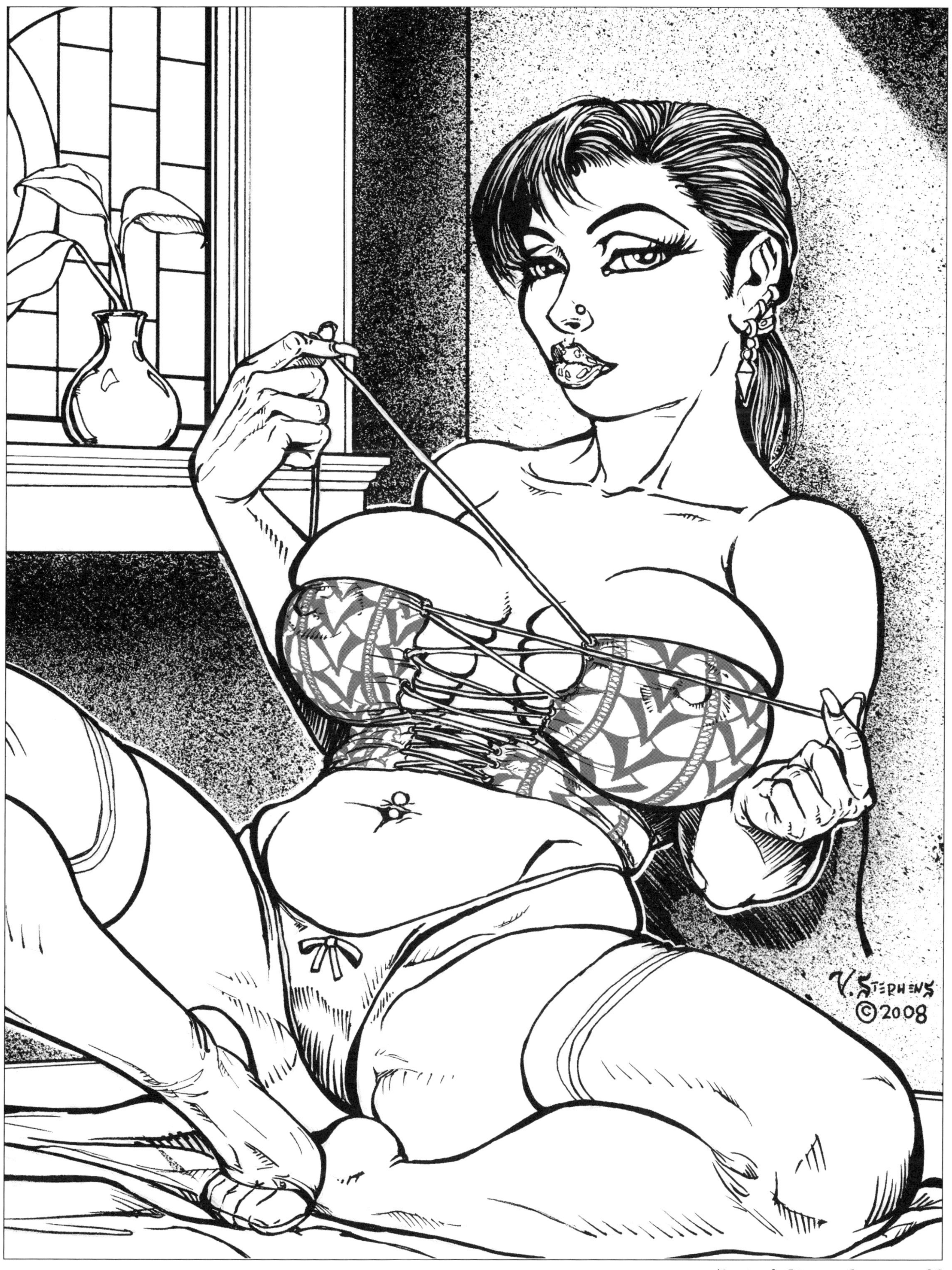
V. STEPHENS
©2008

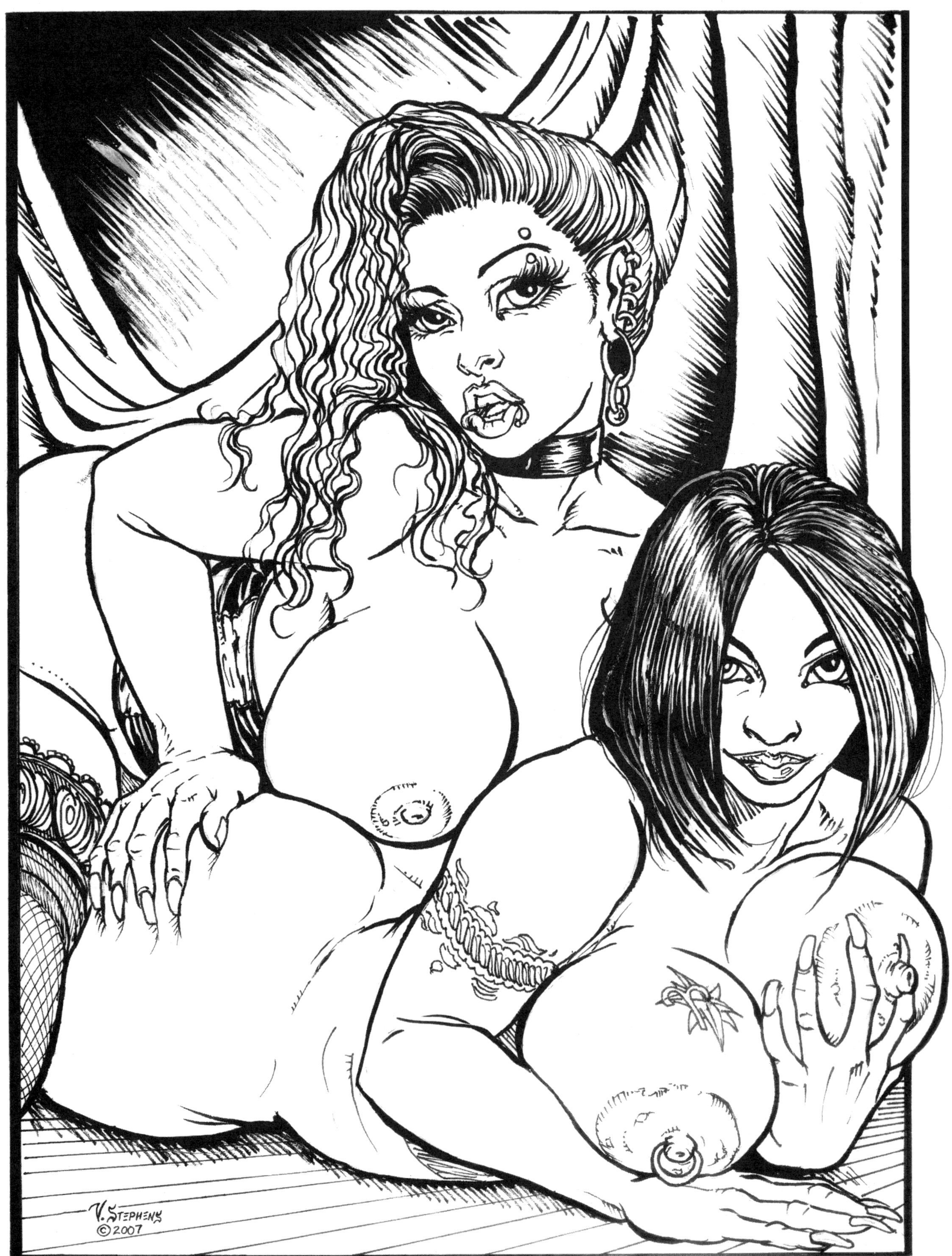
V. STEPHENS
©2007

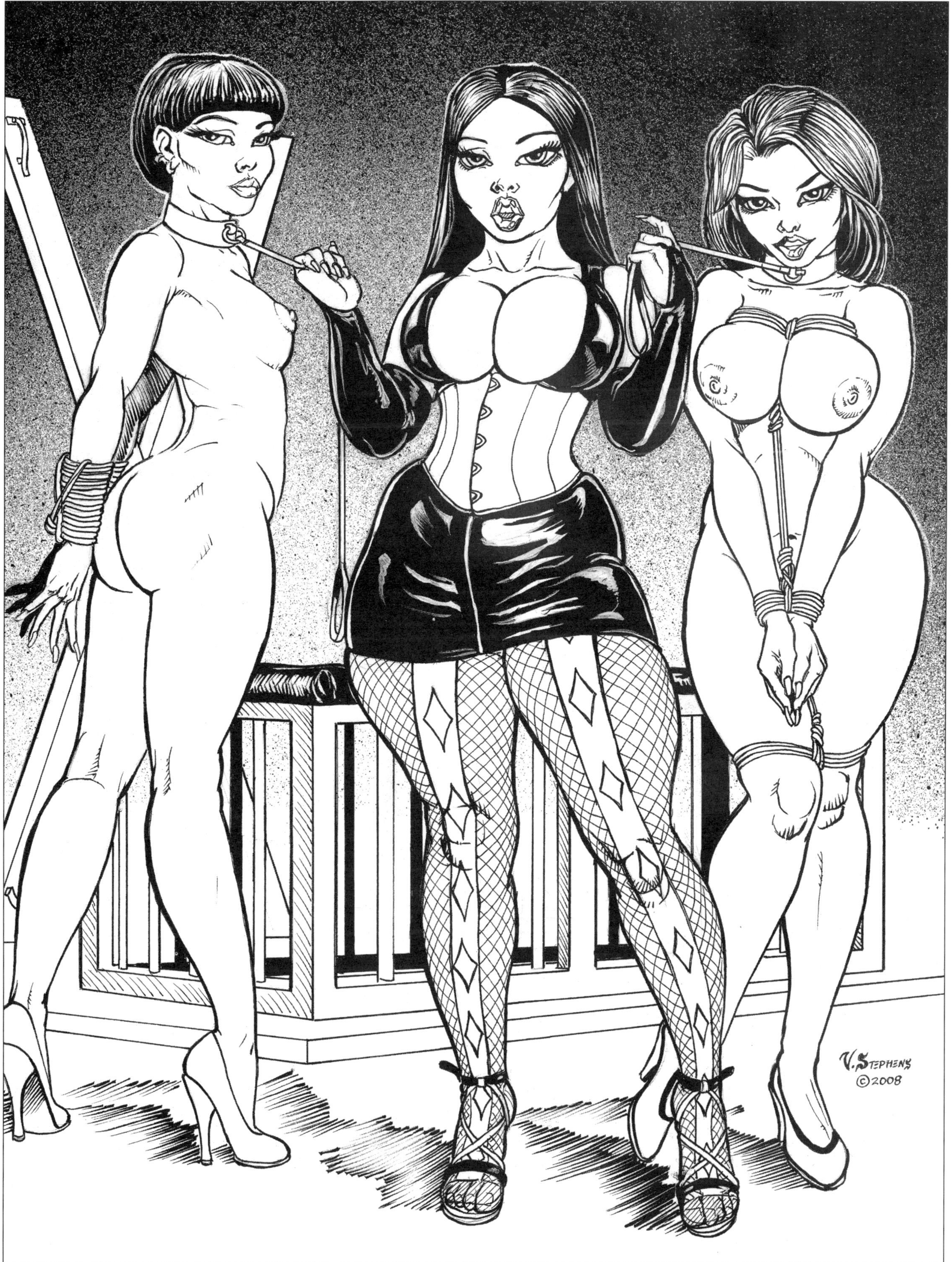
V. STEPHENS
©2008

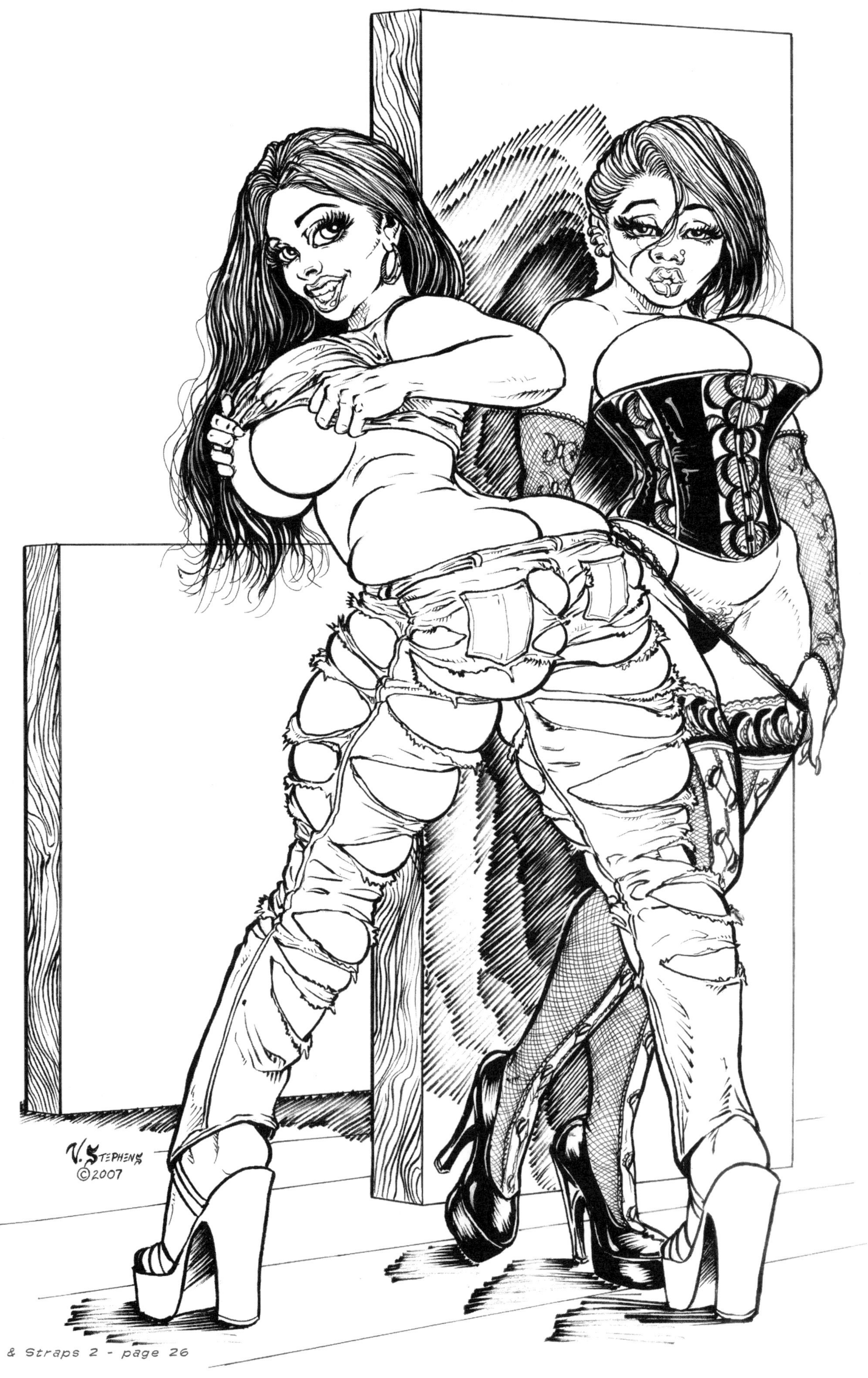
V. Stephens
©2007

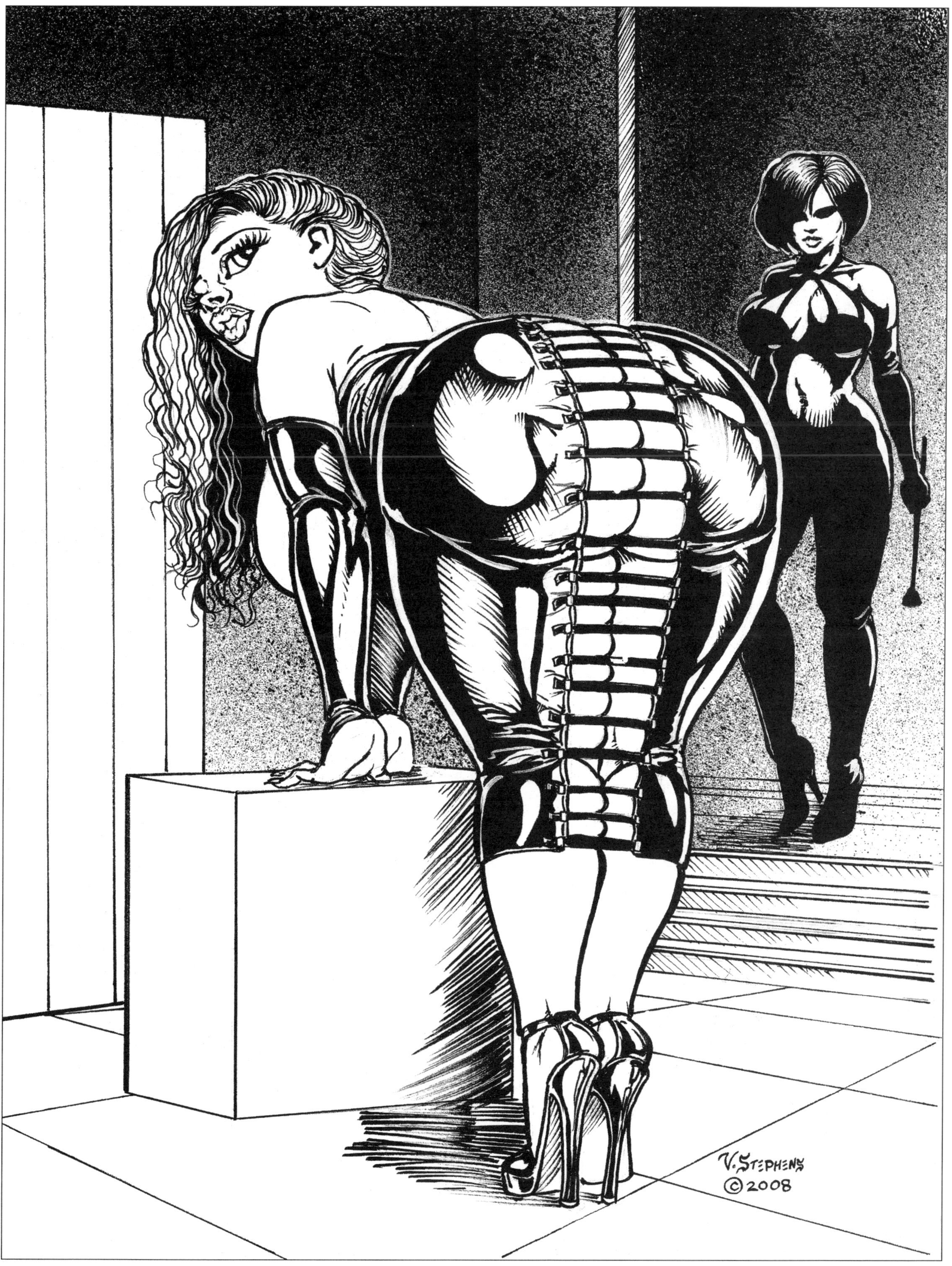
V. STEPHENS
©2008

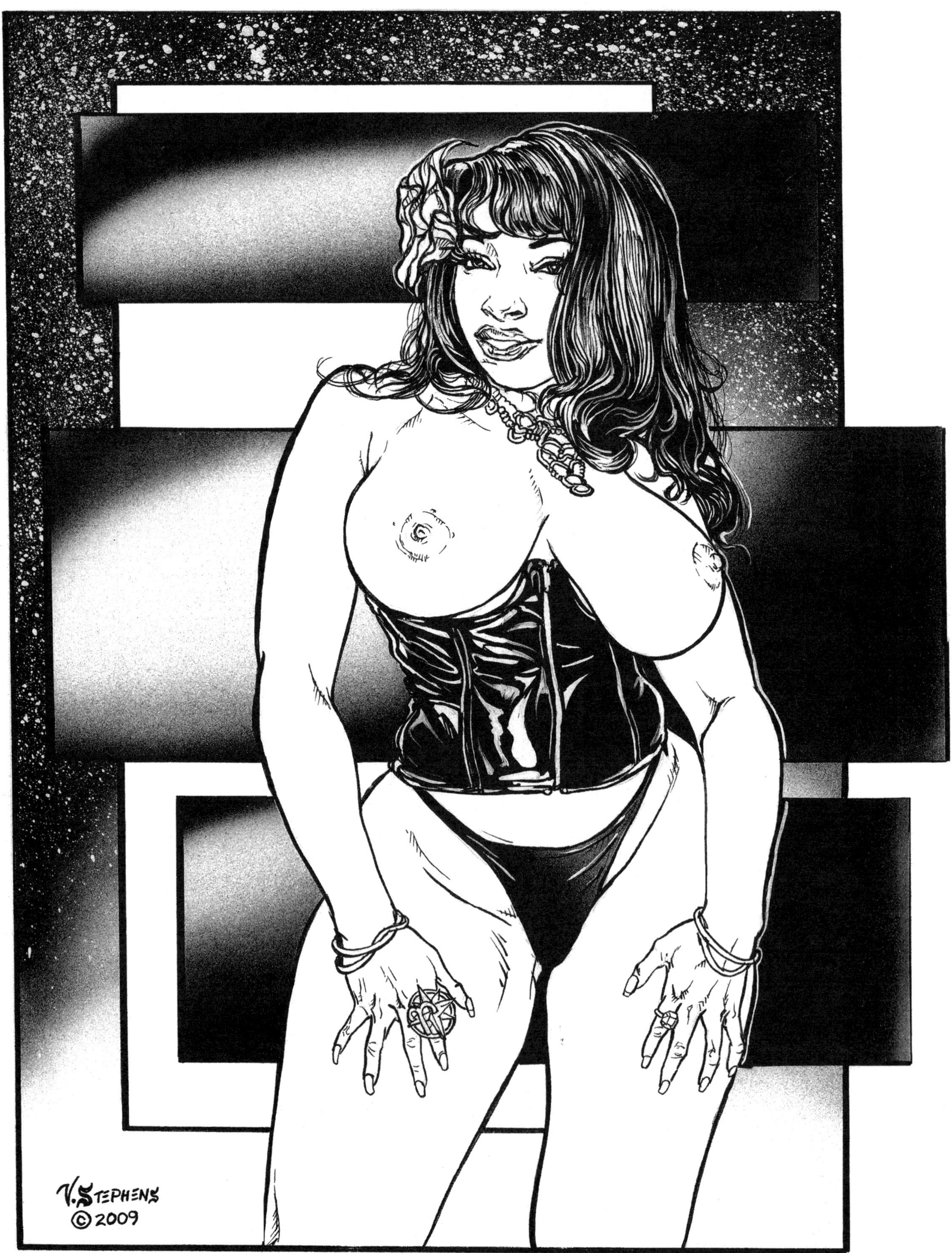
V.STEPHENS
©2009

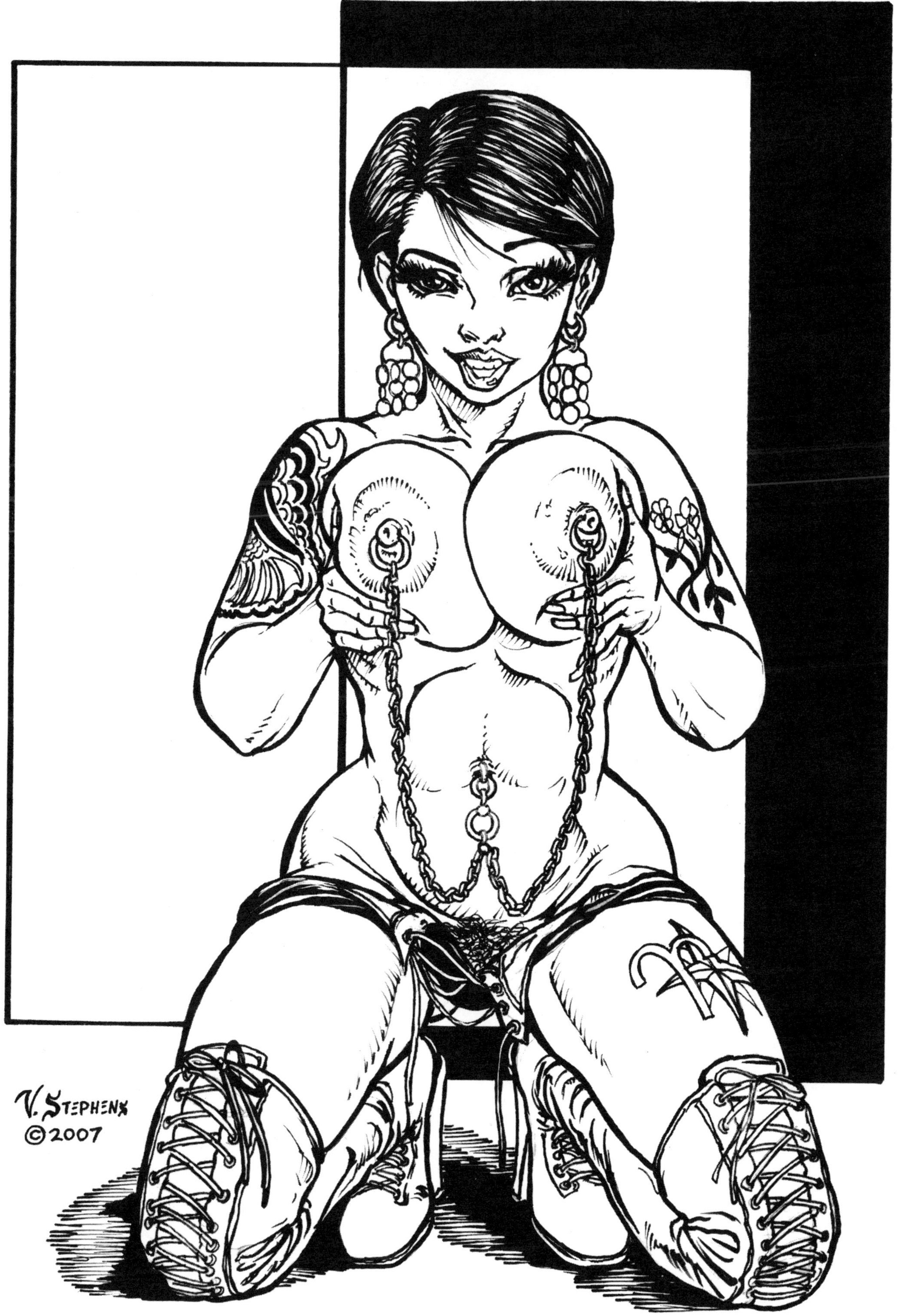
V. Stephens
©2007

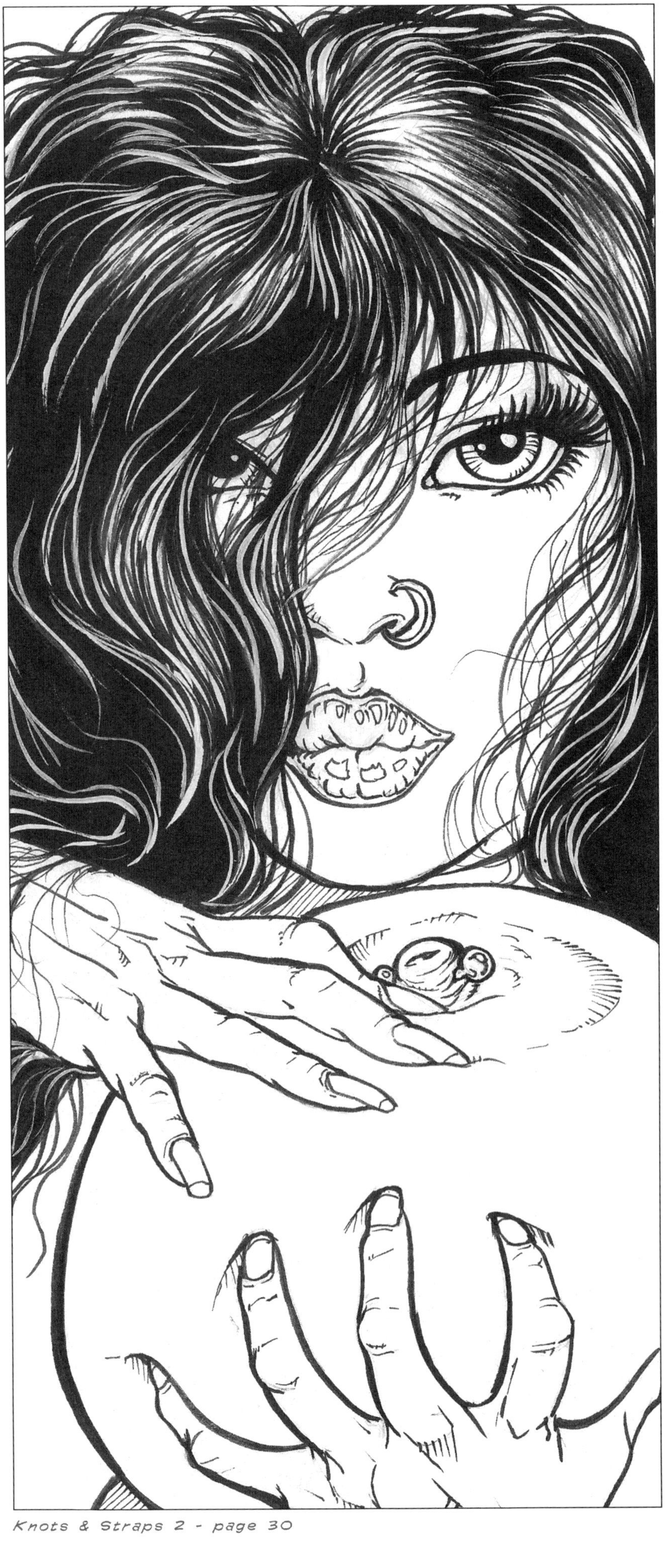

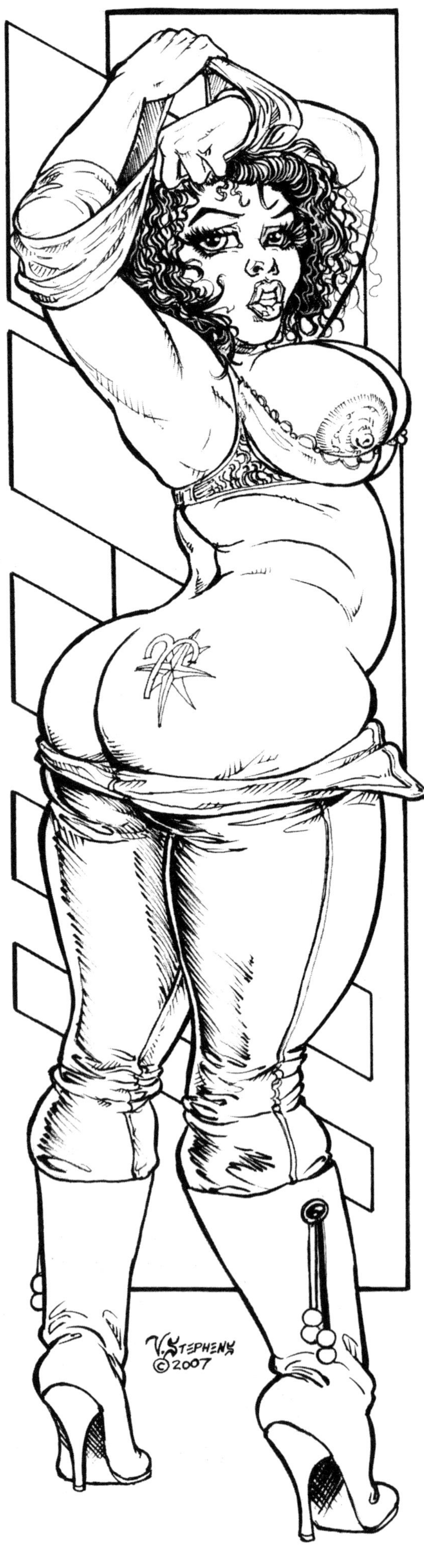
V. Stephens
©2007

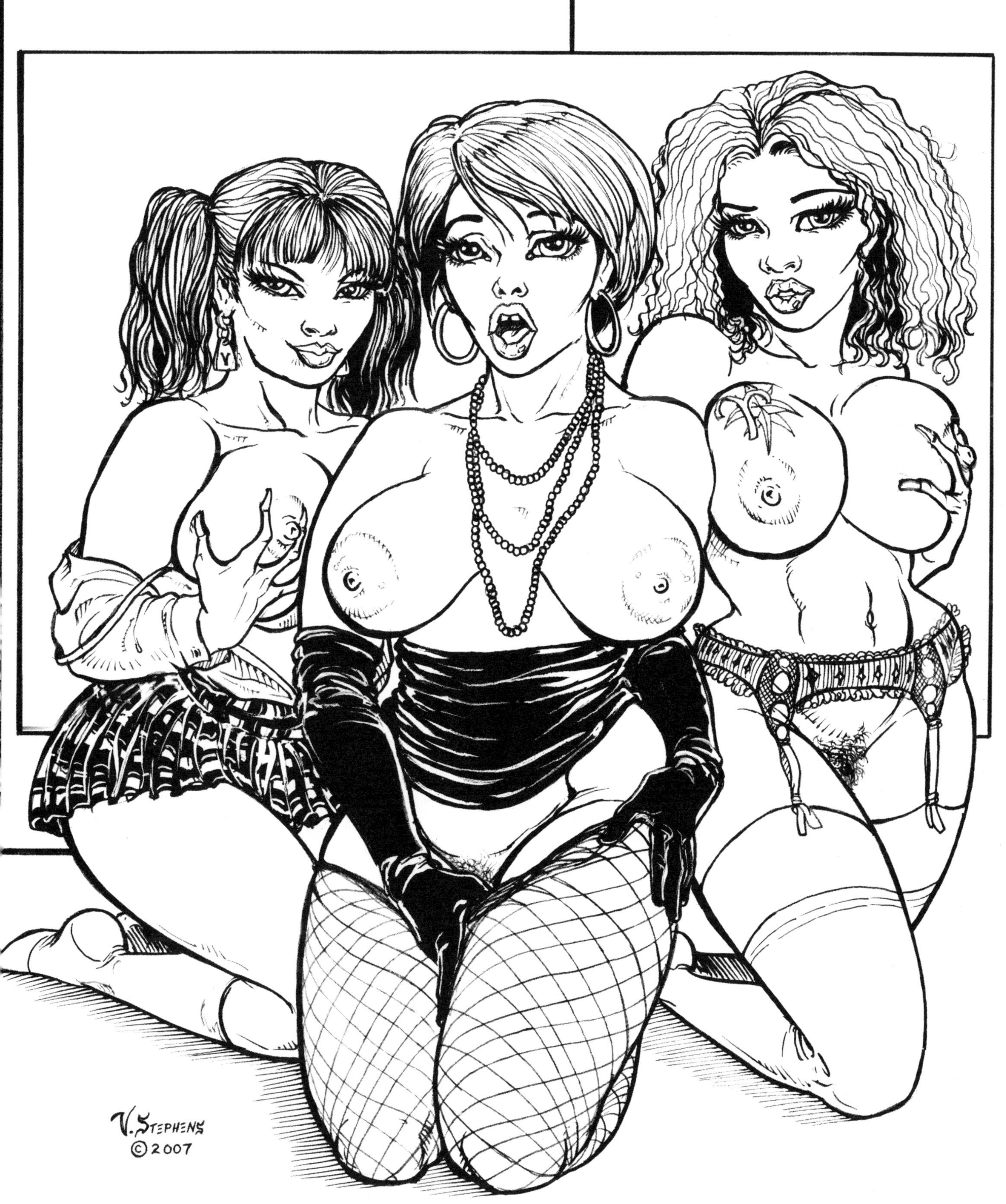
V. STEPHENS
©2007

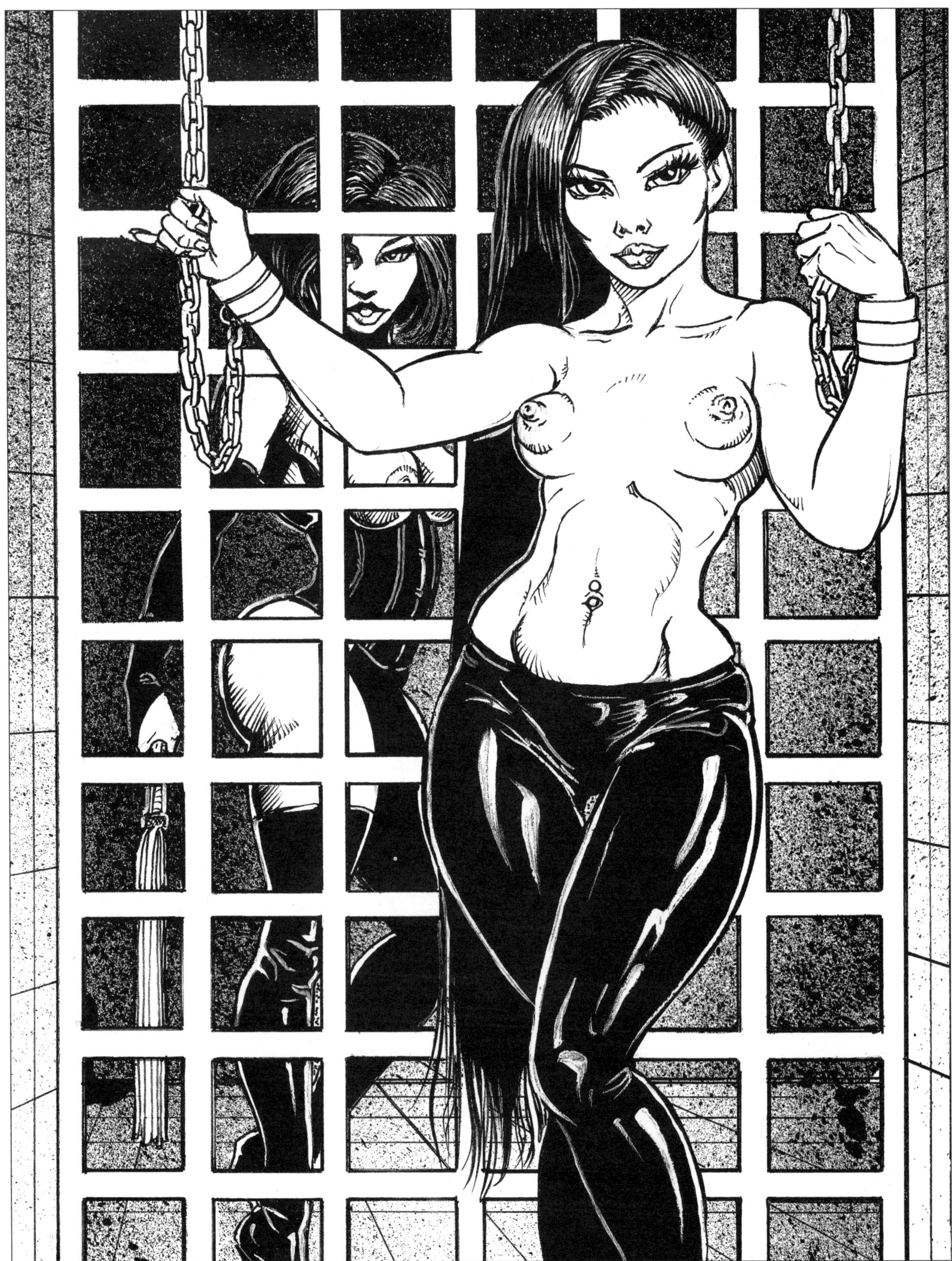

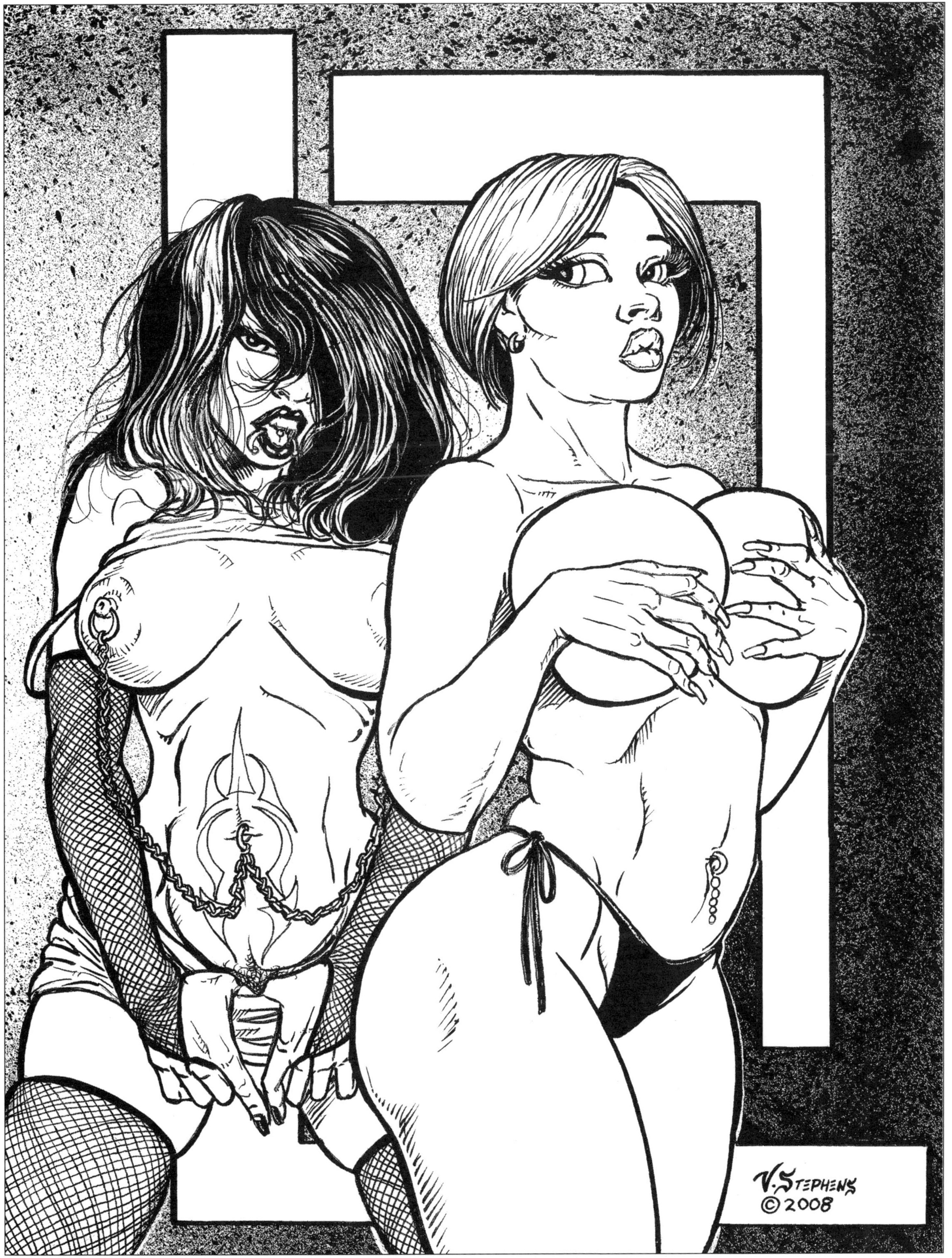
V. STEPHENS
©2008

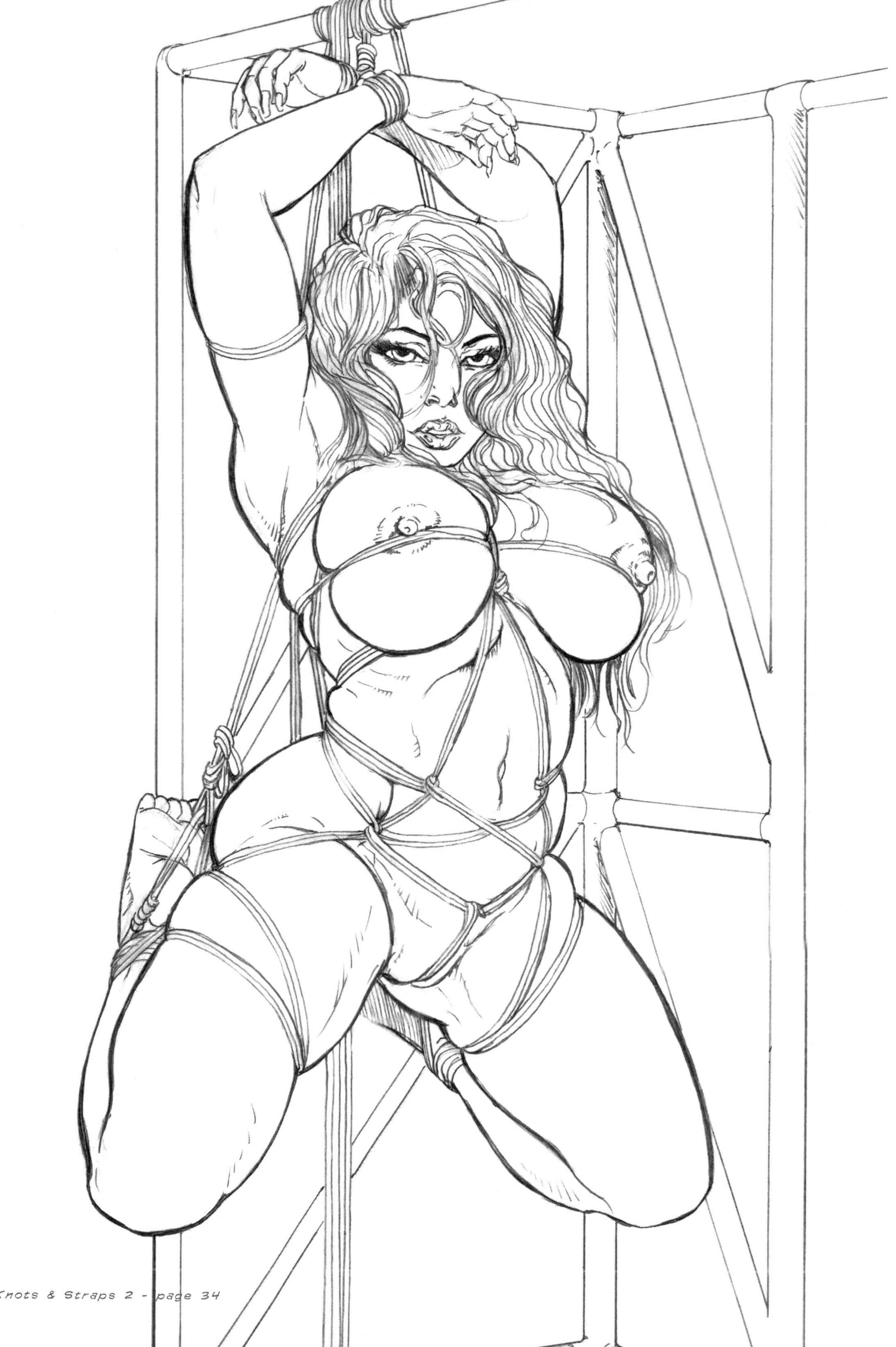

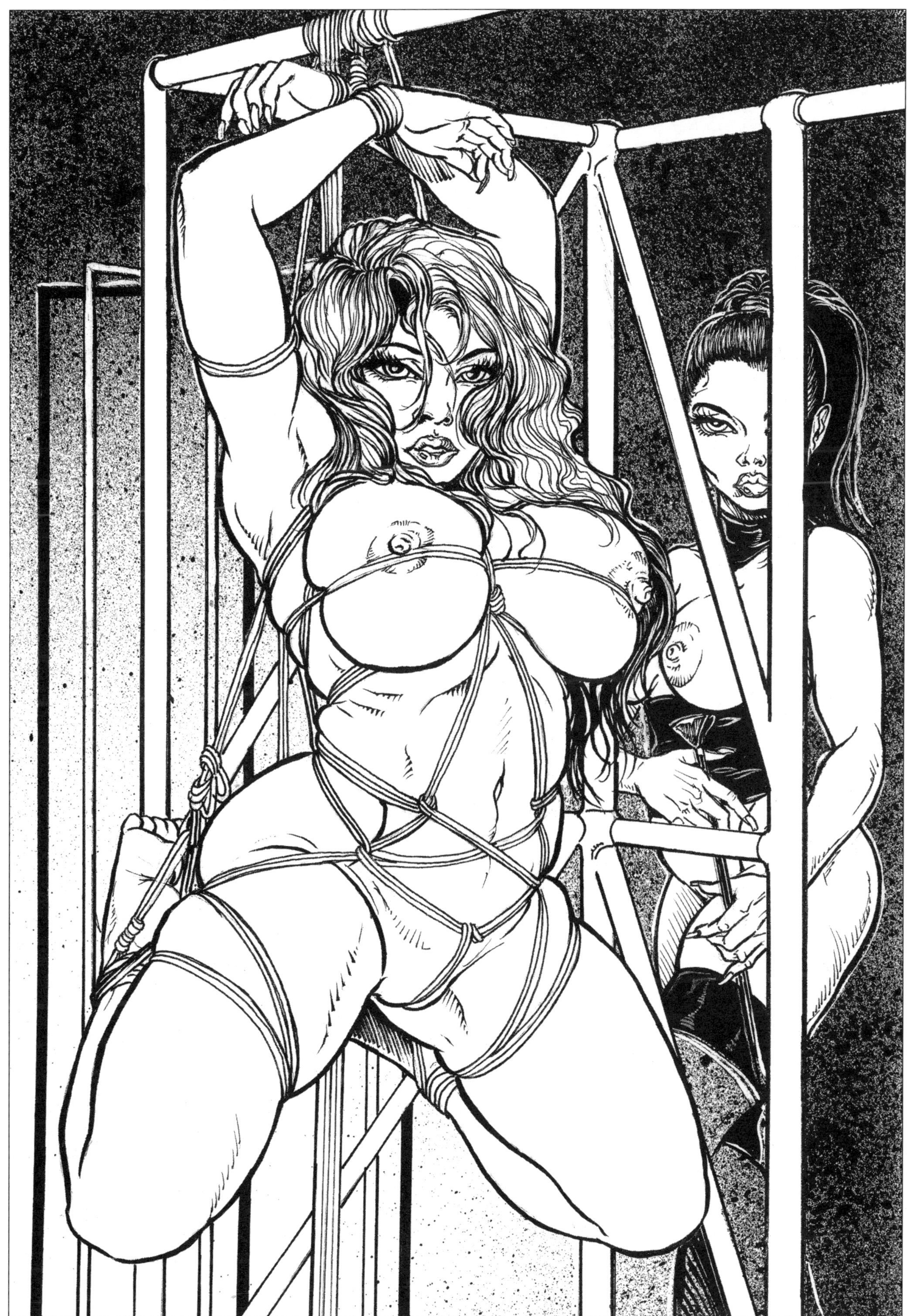

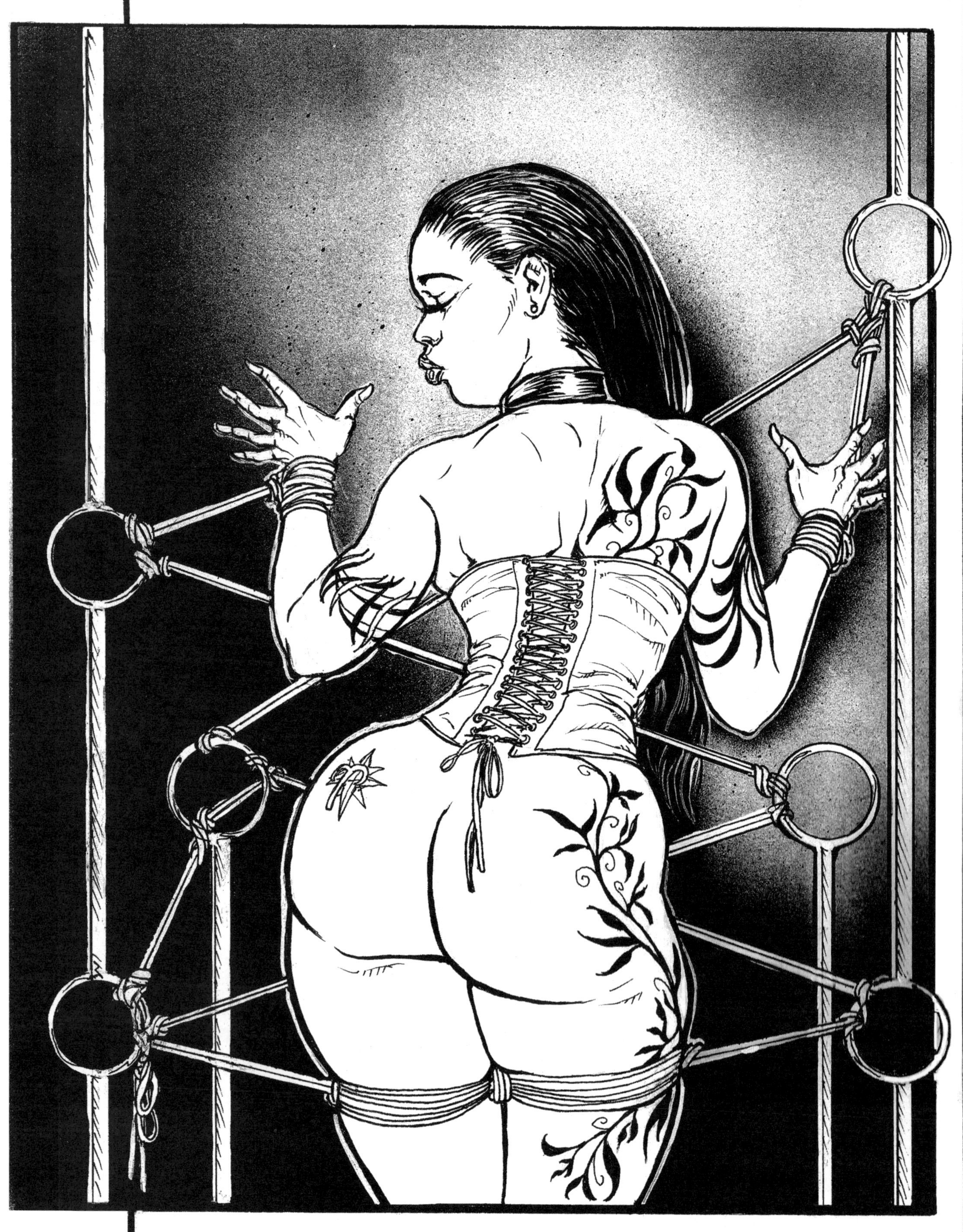
V. STEPHENS
©2009

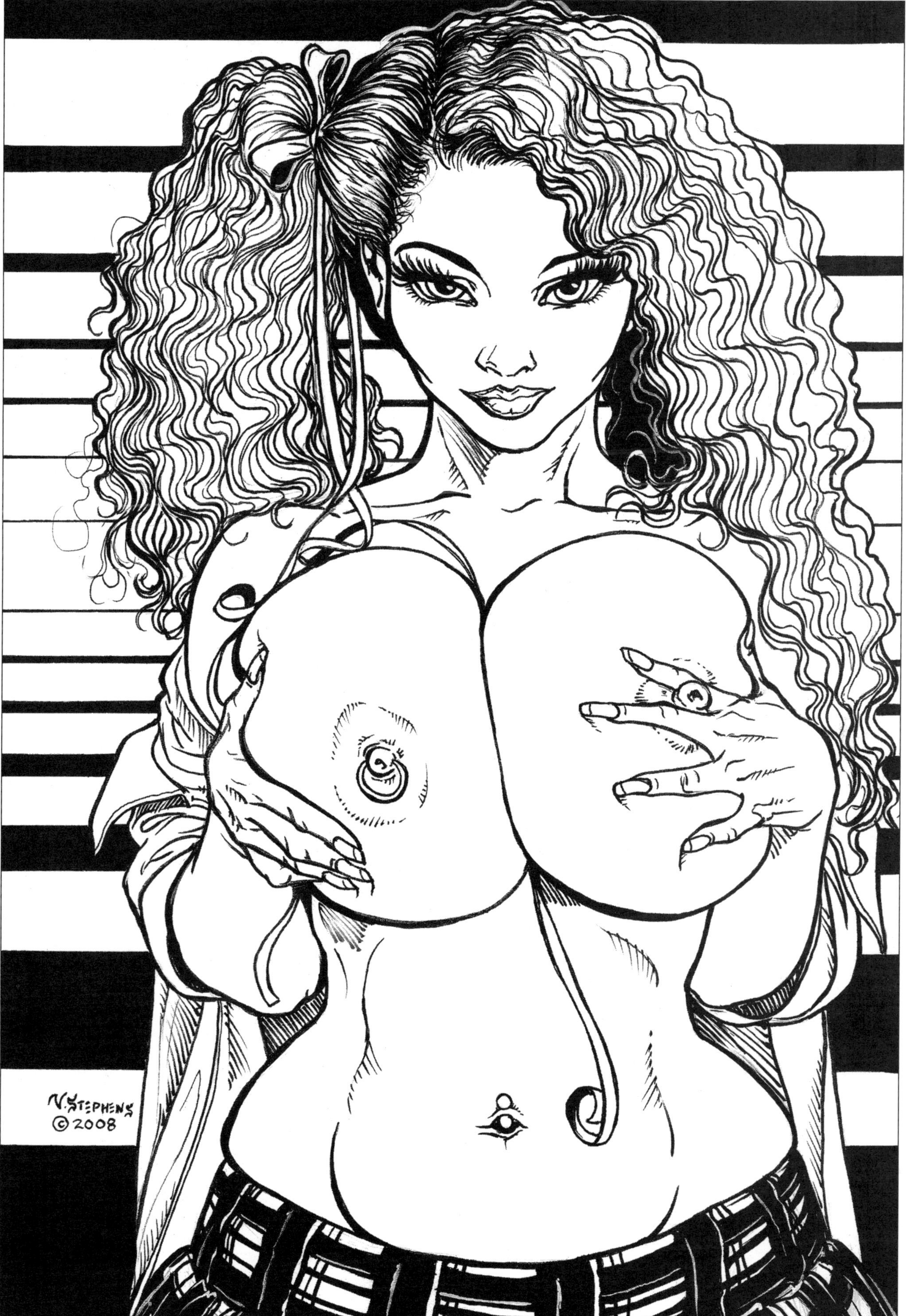
N.STEPHENS
©2008

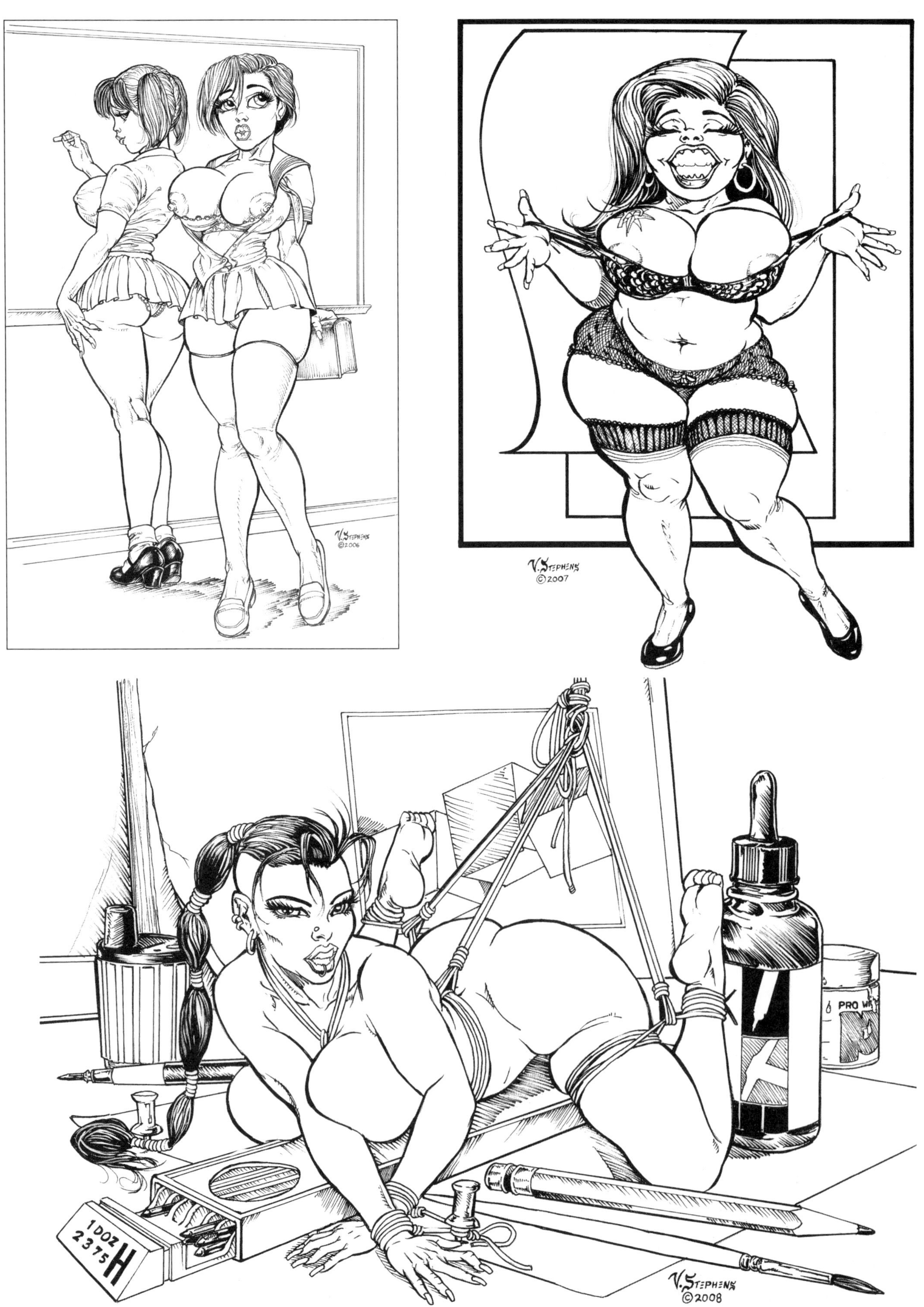
V. Stephens
©2006
V. Stephens
©2007
1 DOZ
2375
H
V. Stephens
©2008

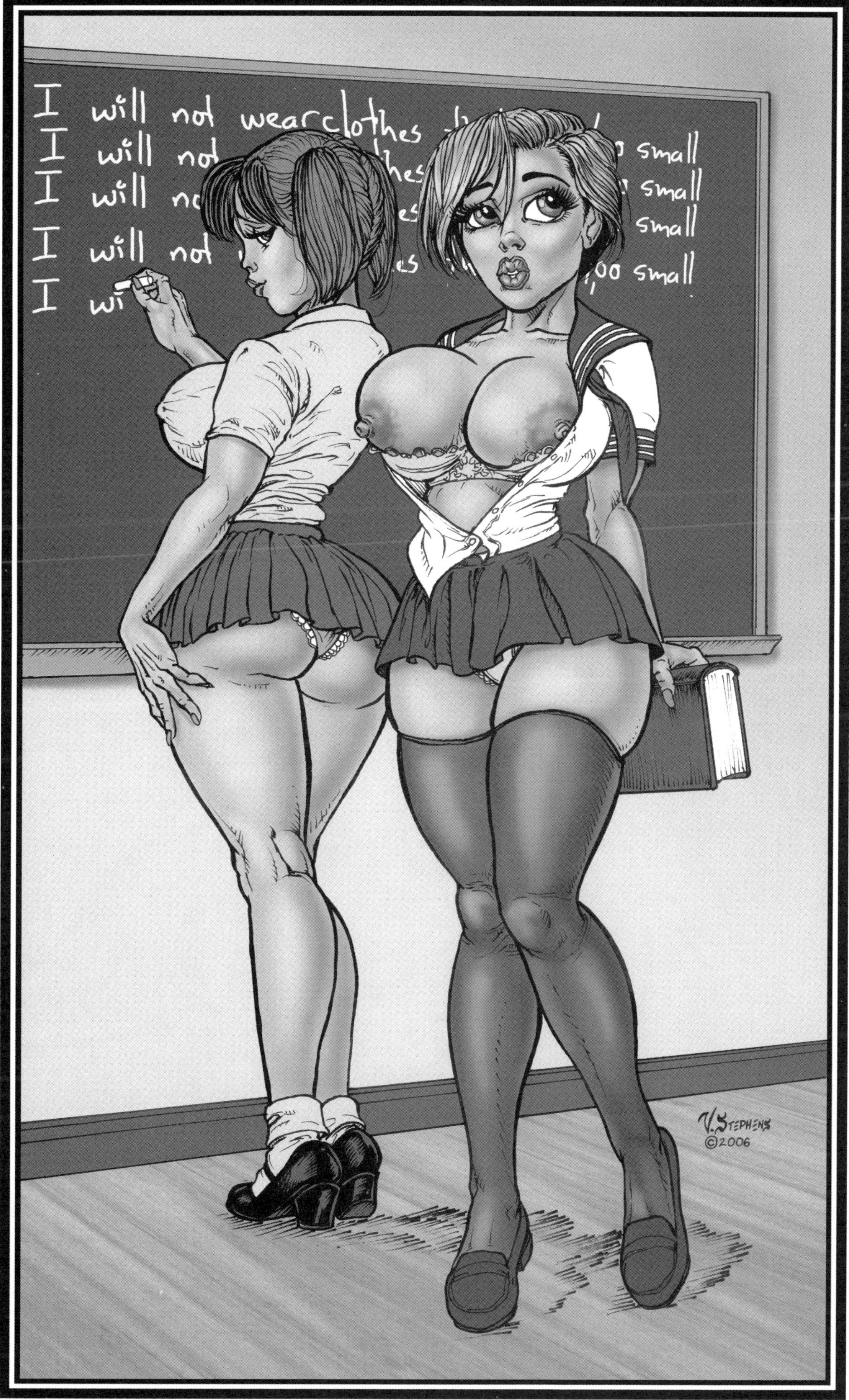
I will not wearclothes
I will no
small
I will no
small
small
I will not
small
V. Stephens
©2006

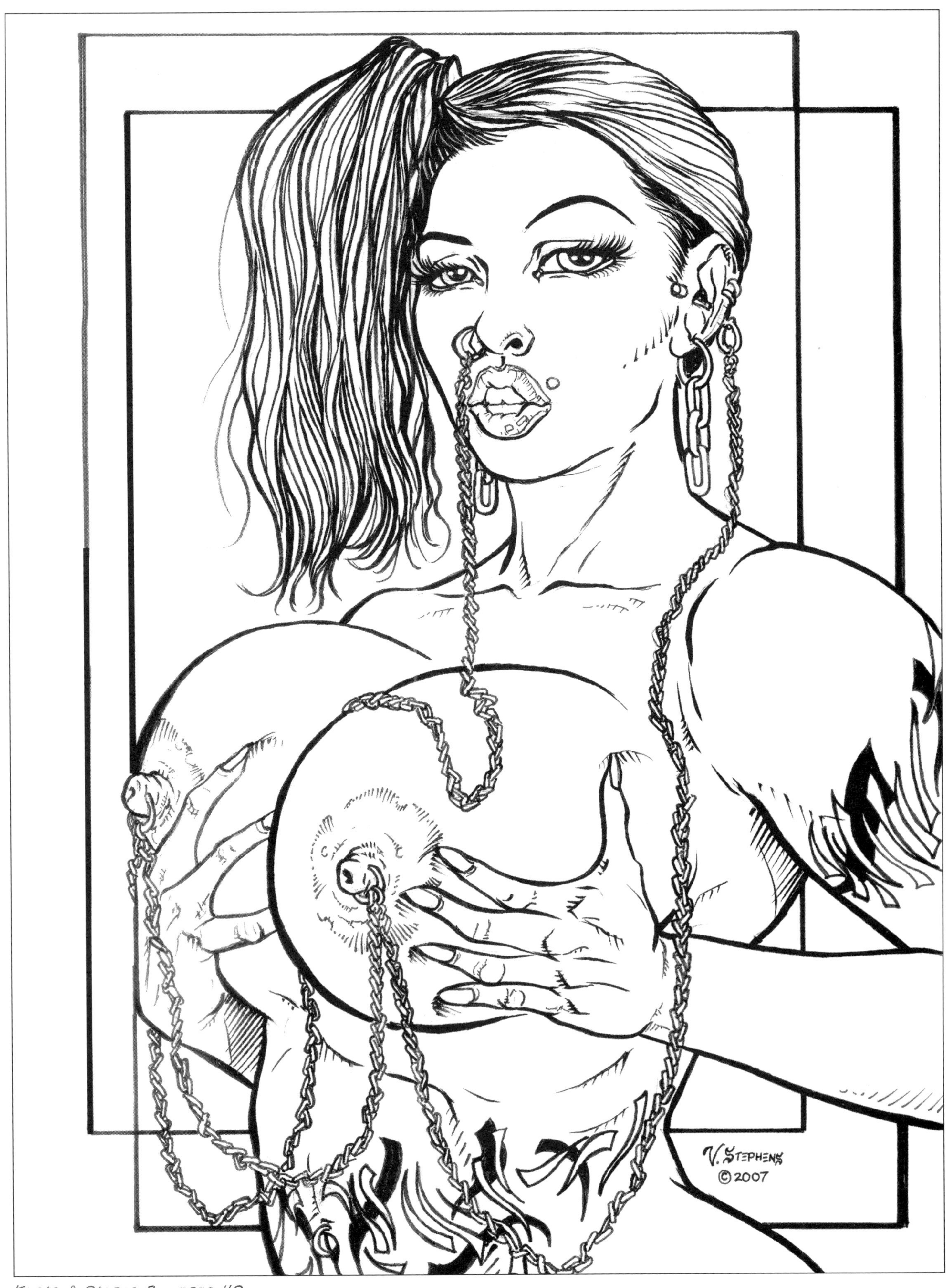
V. STEPHENS
©2007

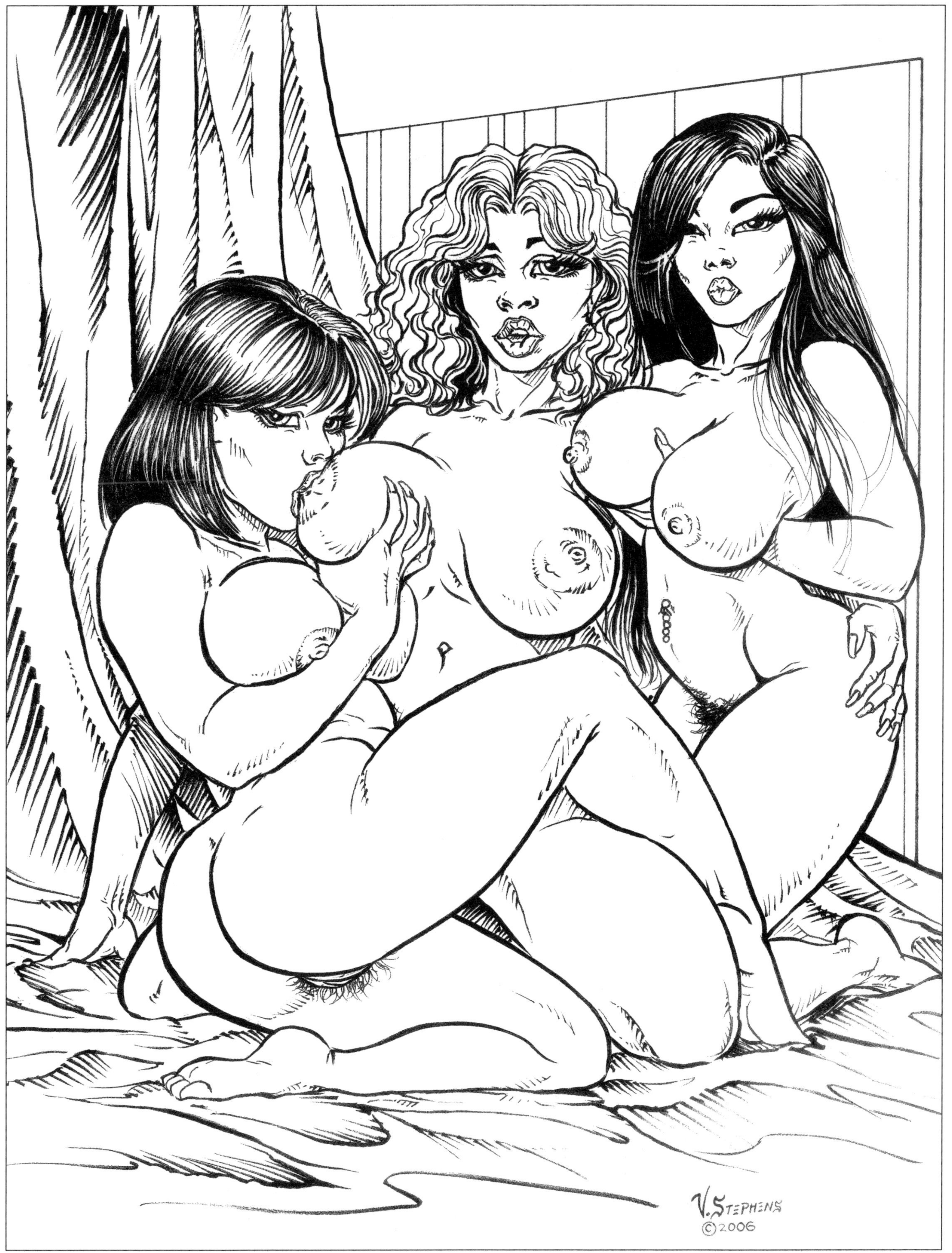
V.STEPHENS
©2006

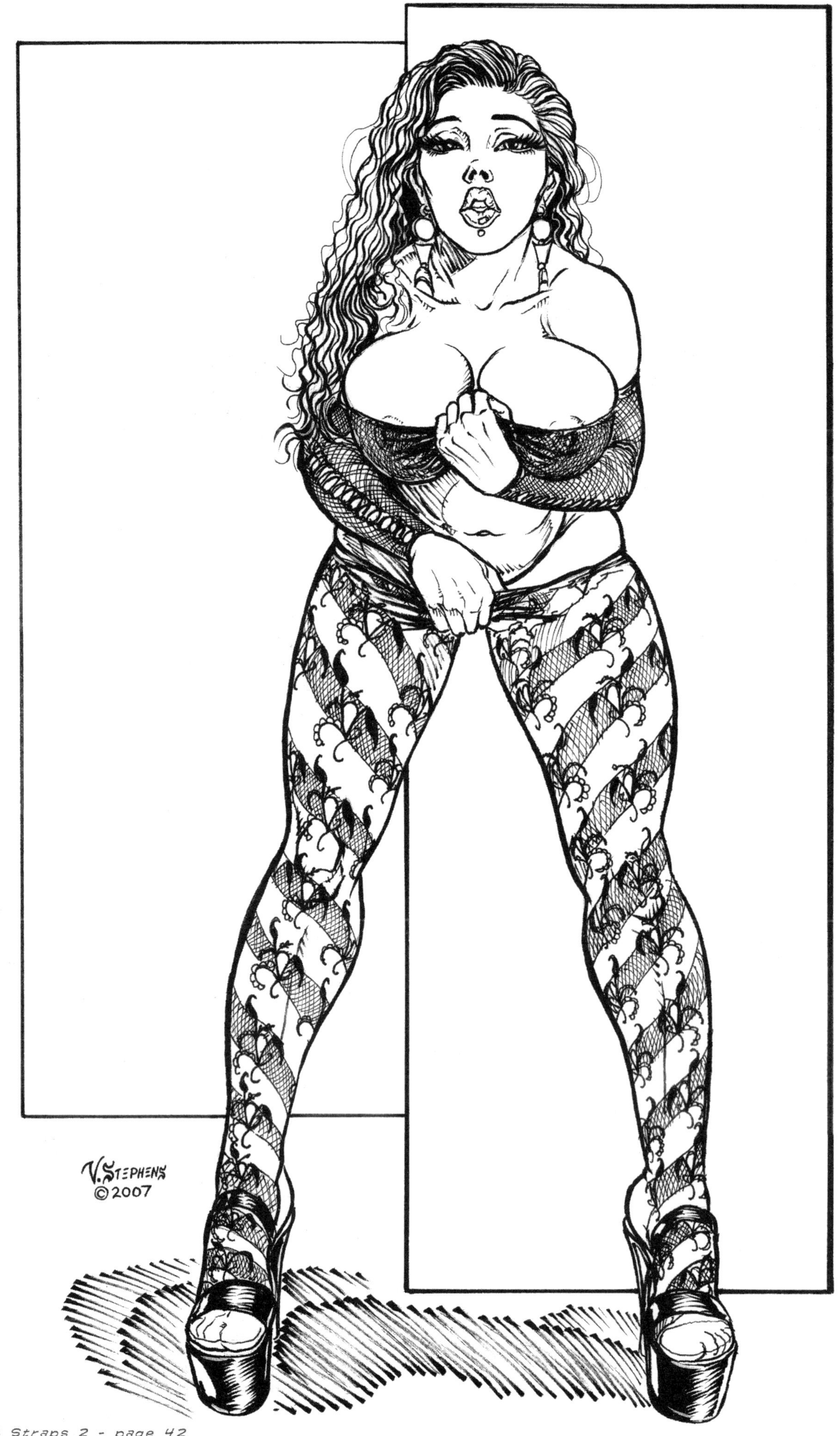
V. STEPHENS
©2007

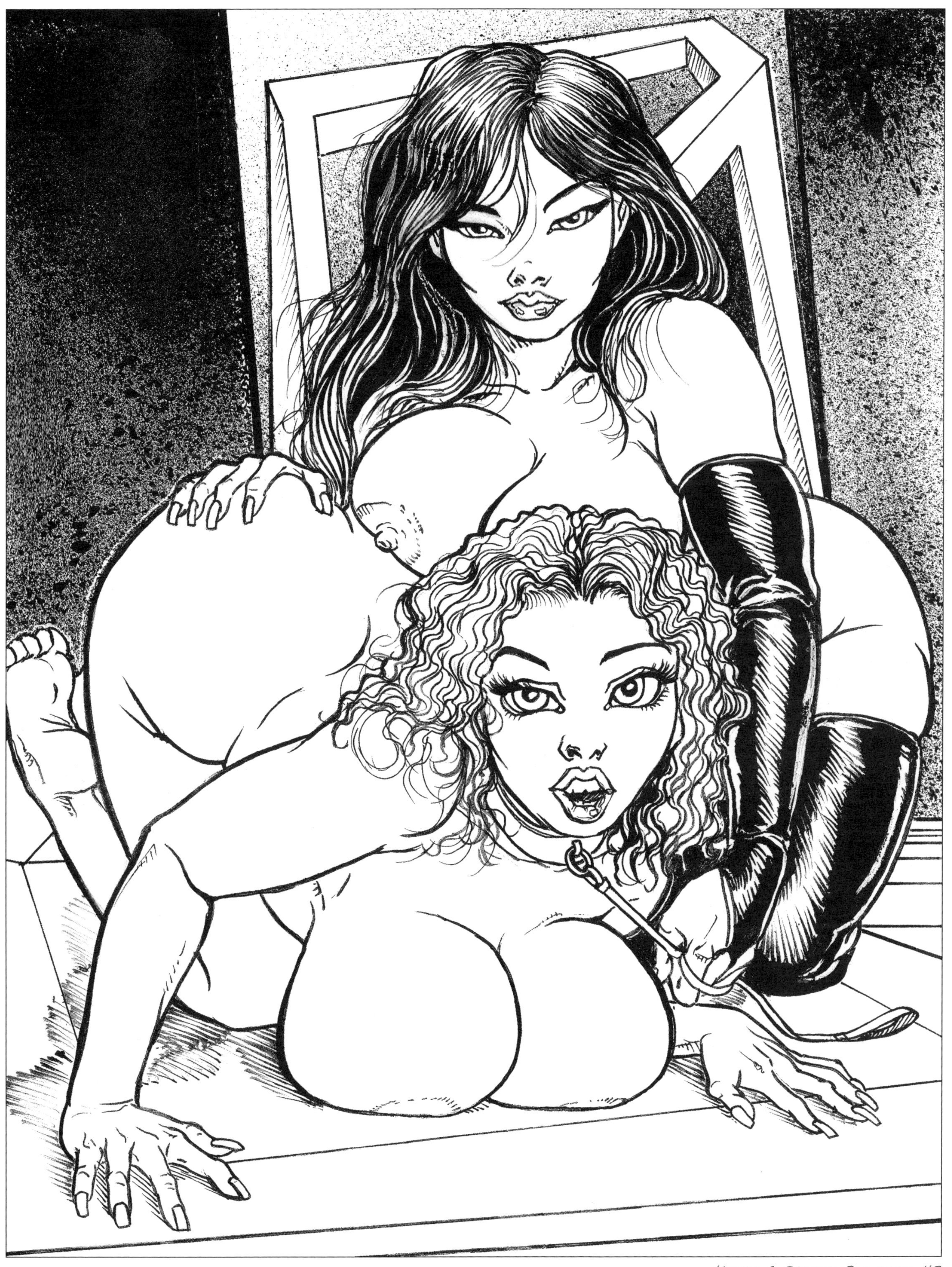

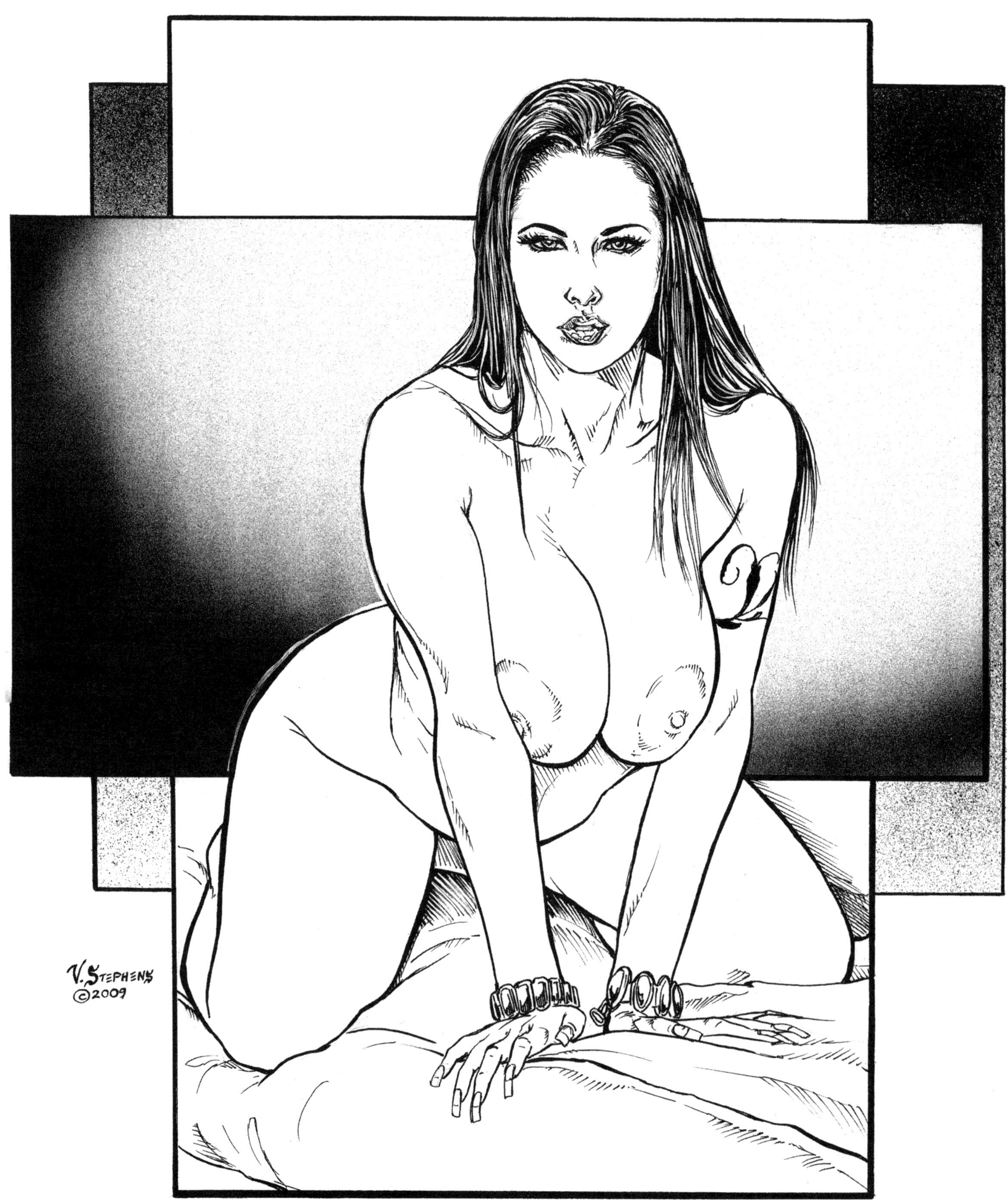
V. STEPHENS
©2009

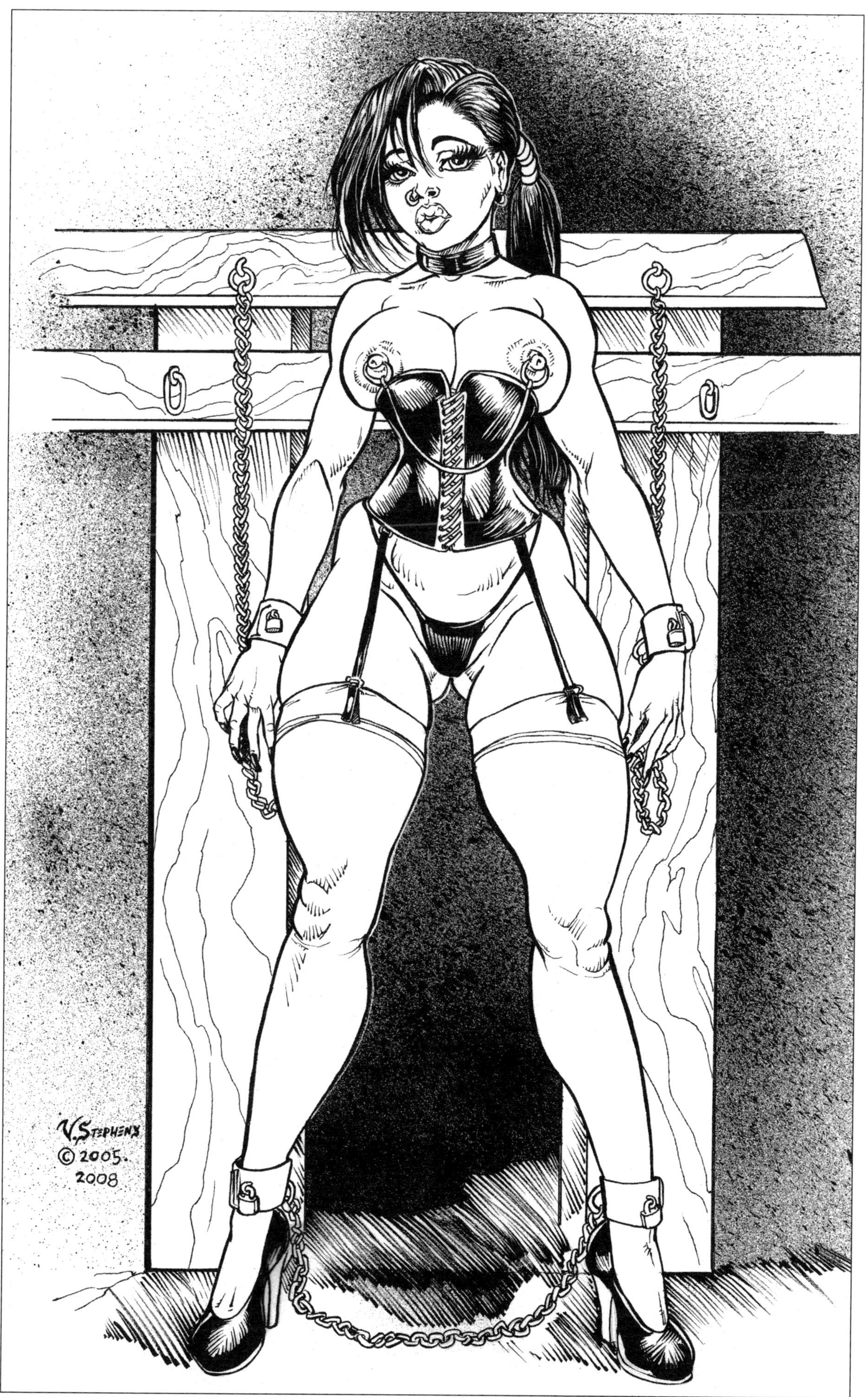
V. Stephens
© 2005.
2008

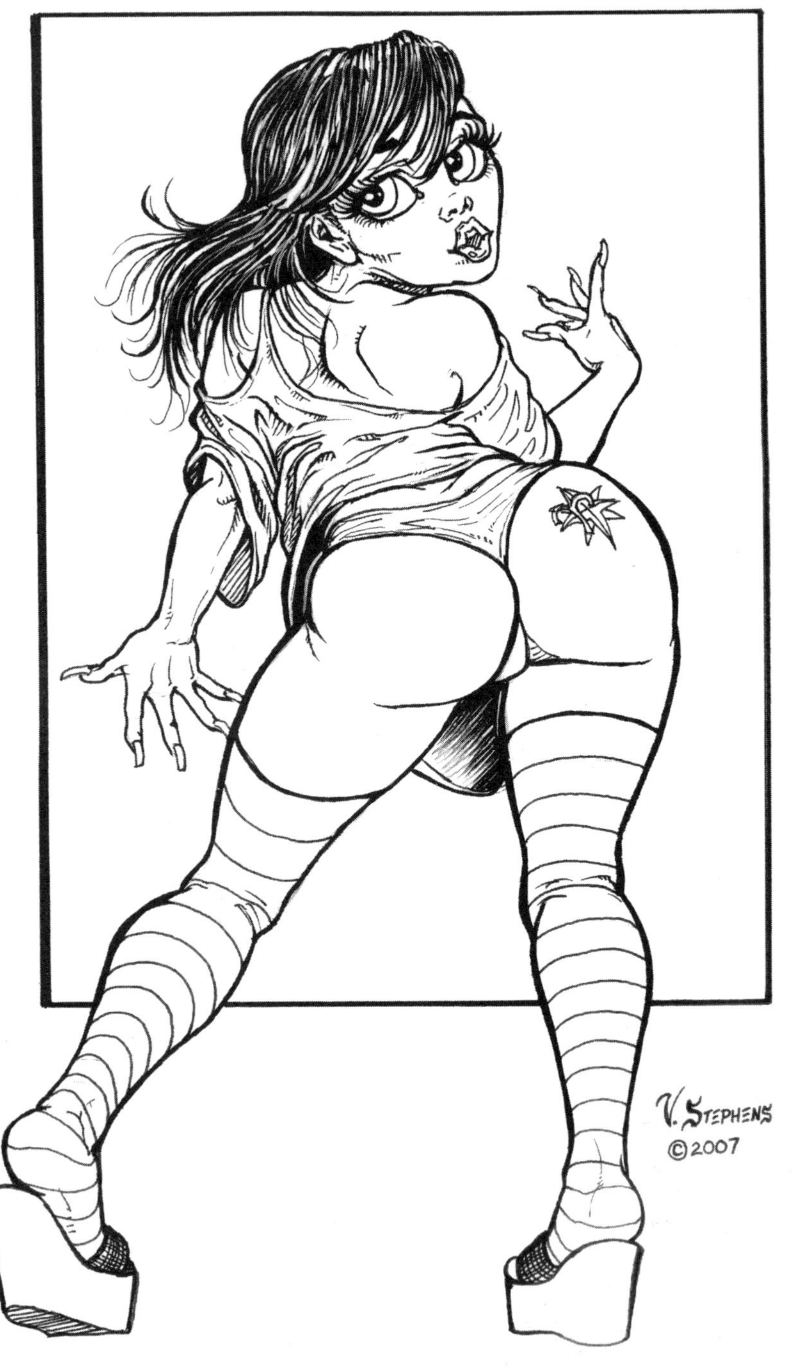
V. STEPHENS
©2007

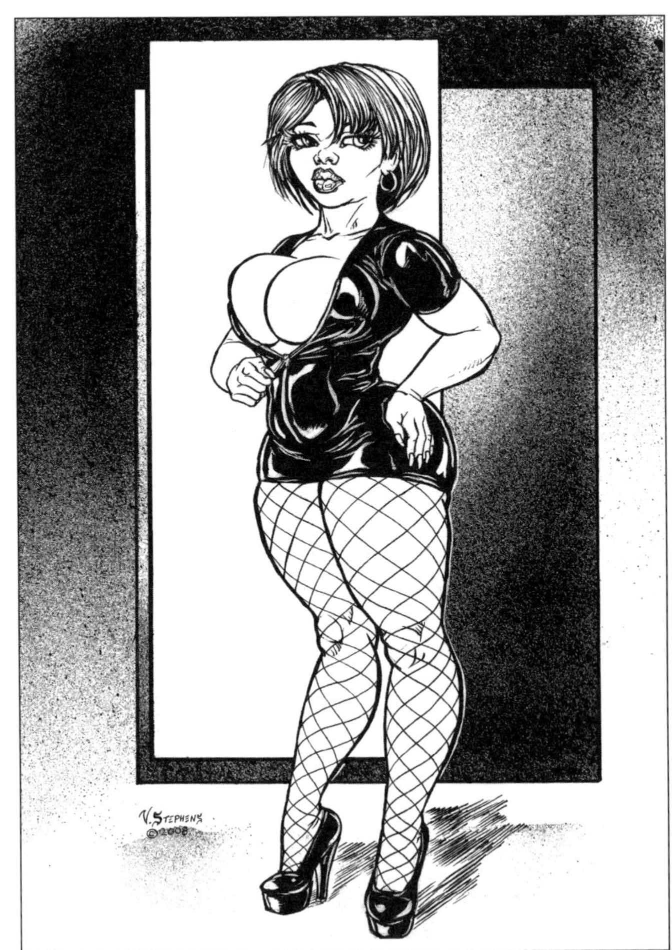
V. STEPHENS

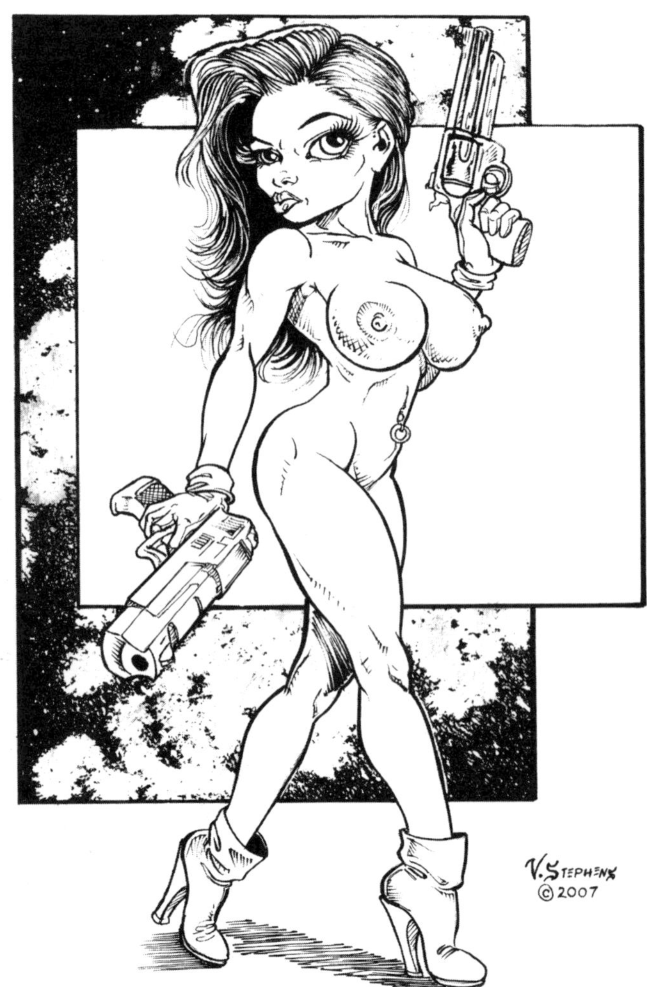
V. STEPHENS
©2007

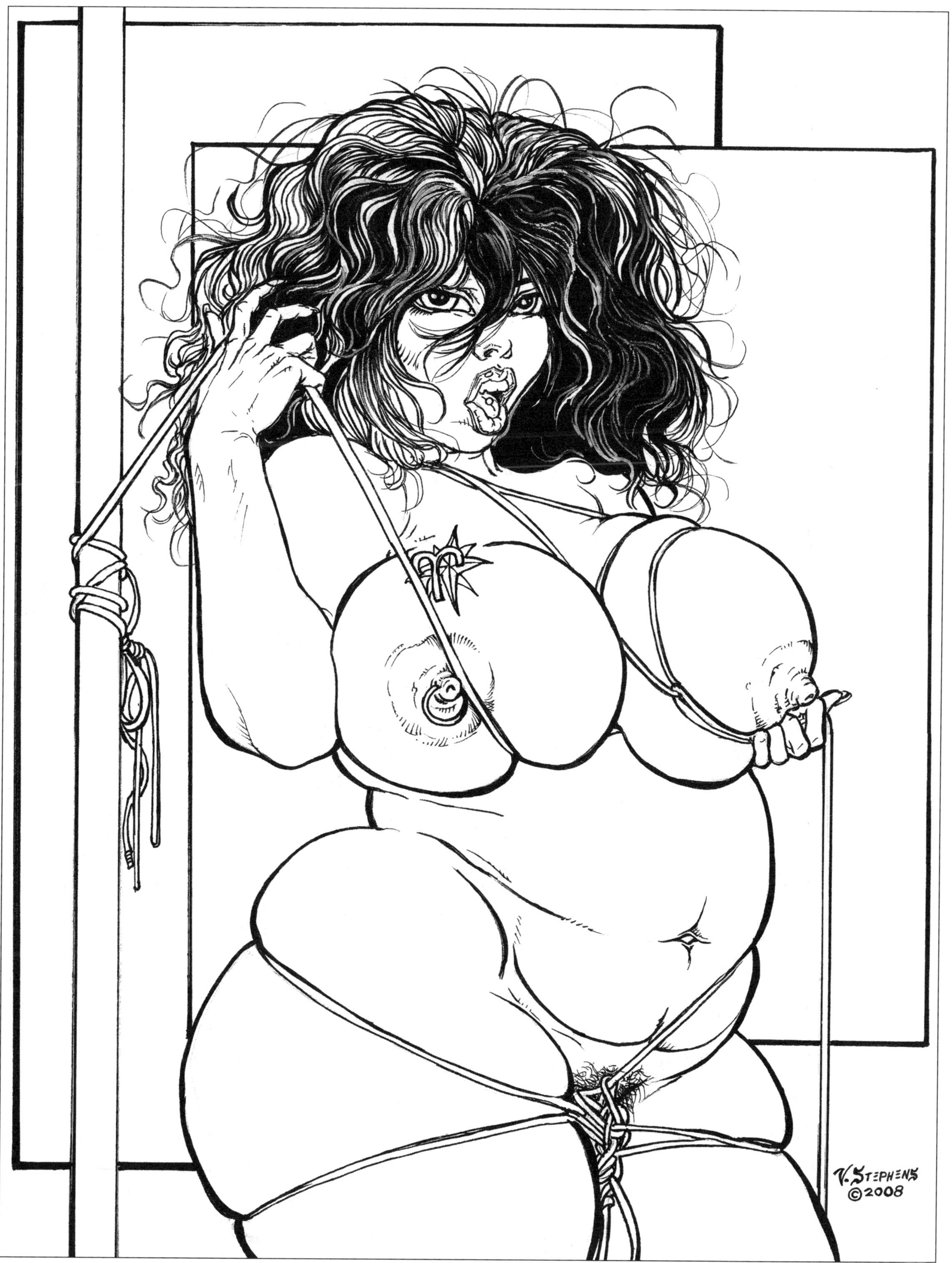
V. STEPHENS
©2008

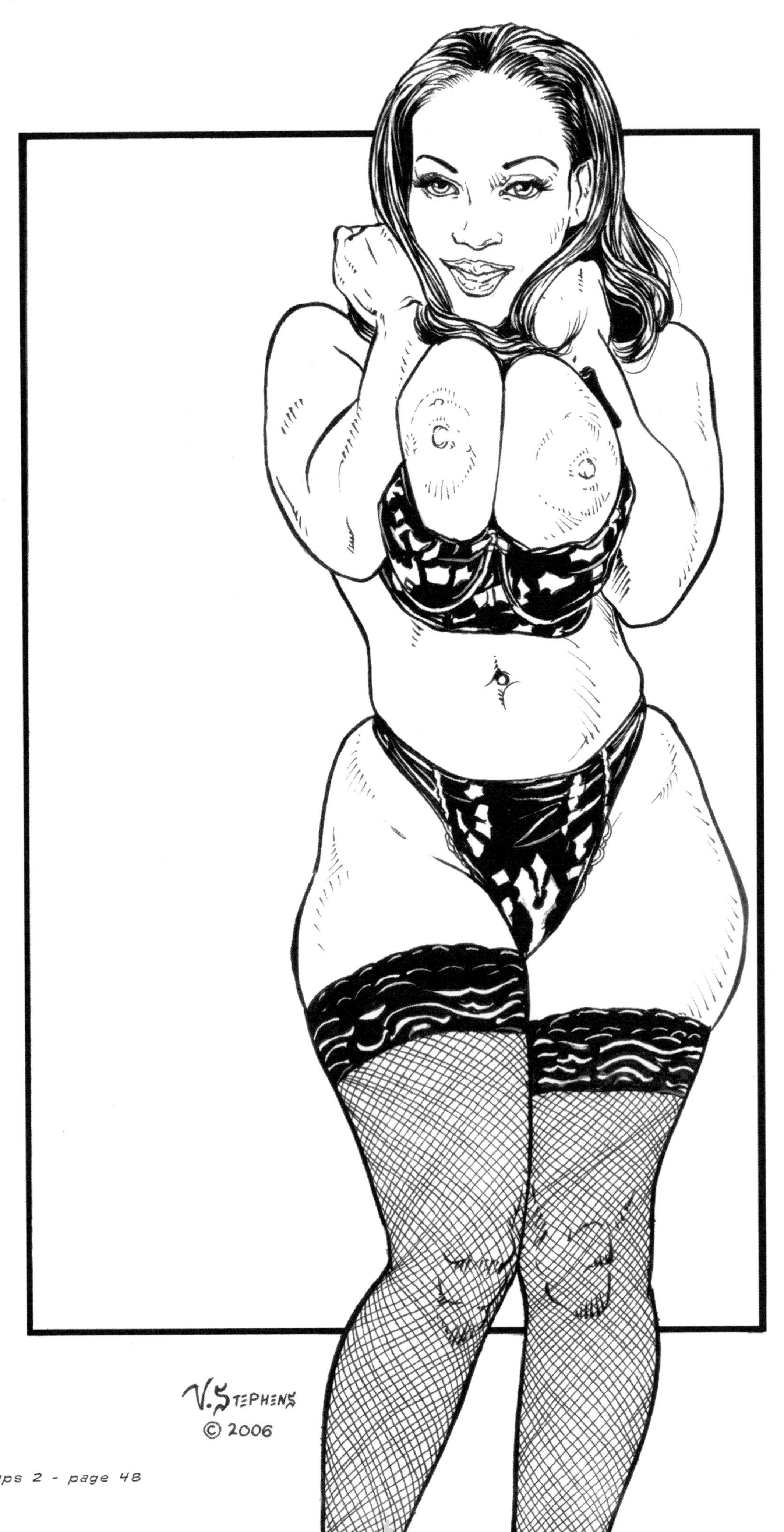
V. STEPHENS
© 2006

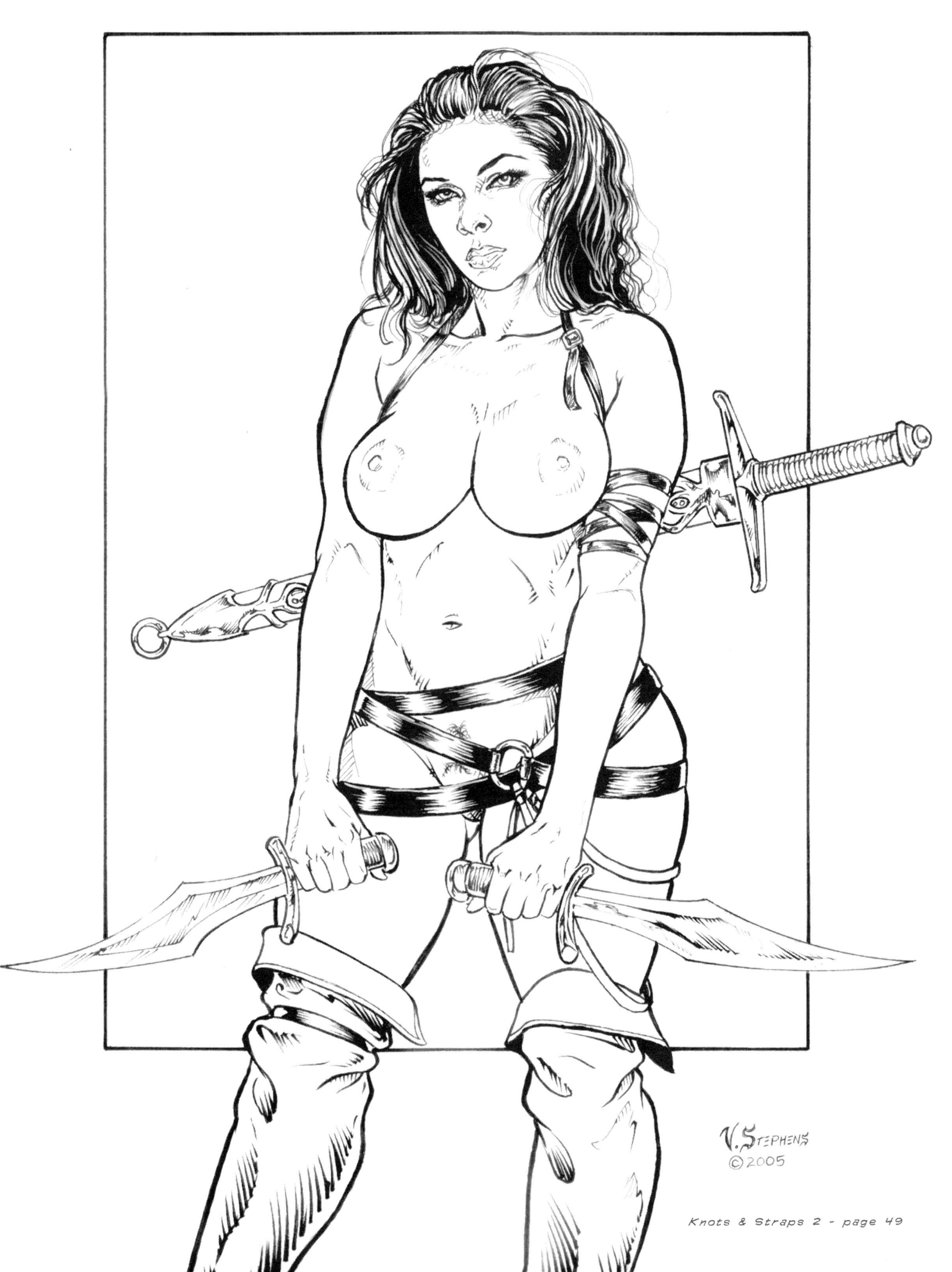
V. STEPHENS
©2005

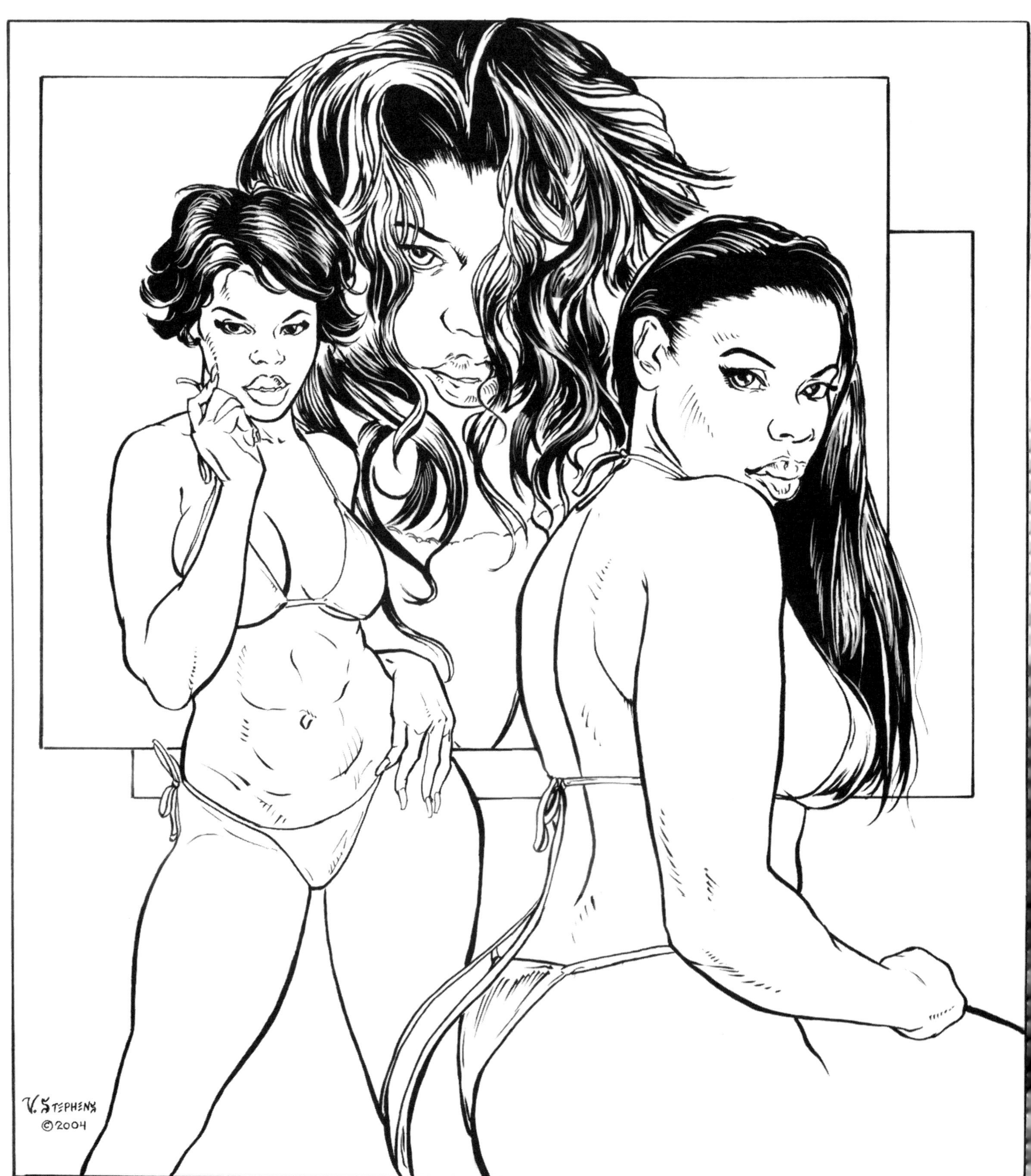
V. STEPHENS
©2004

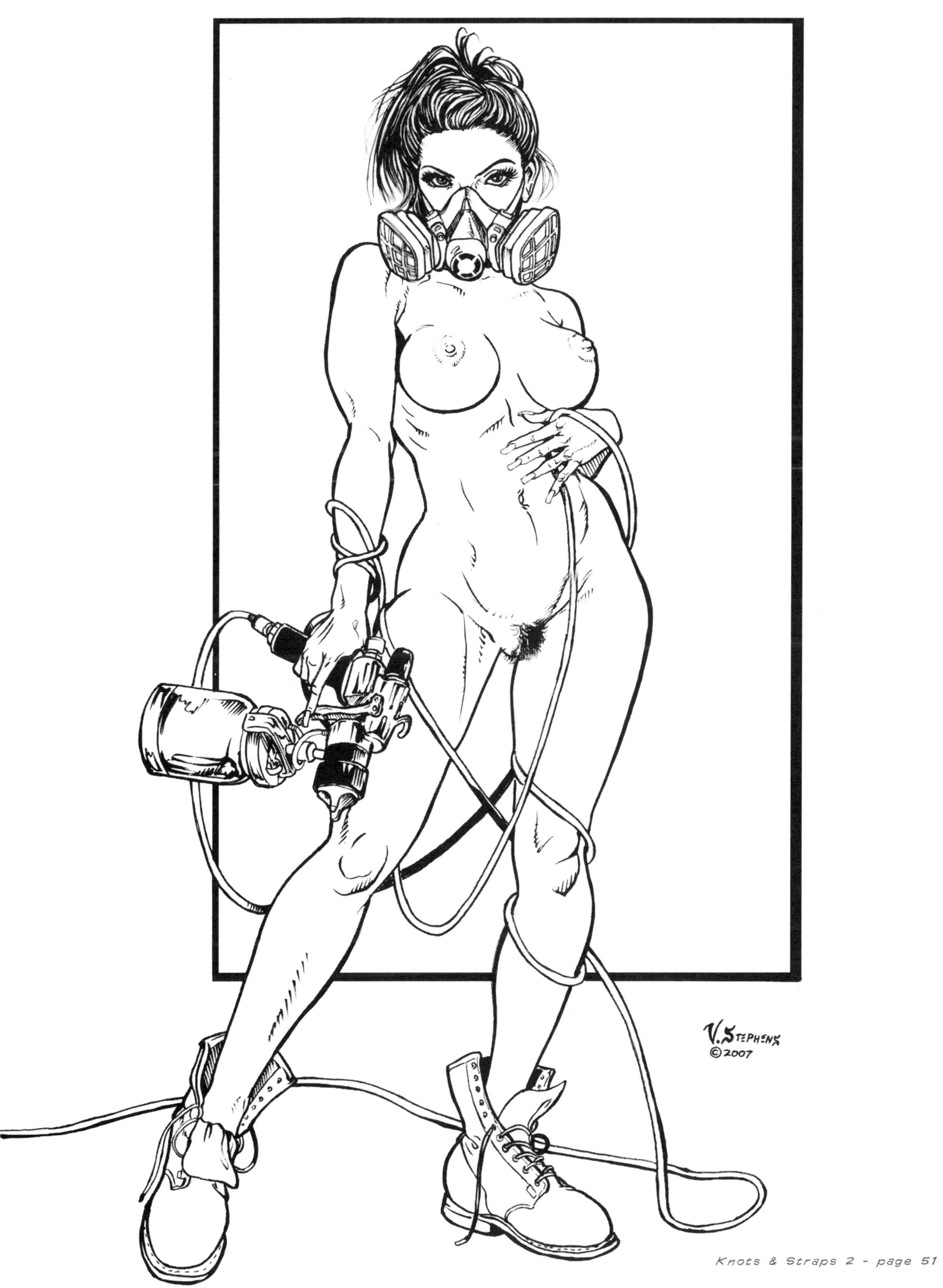
V. Stephens
©2007

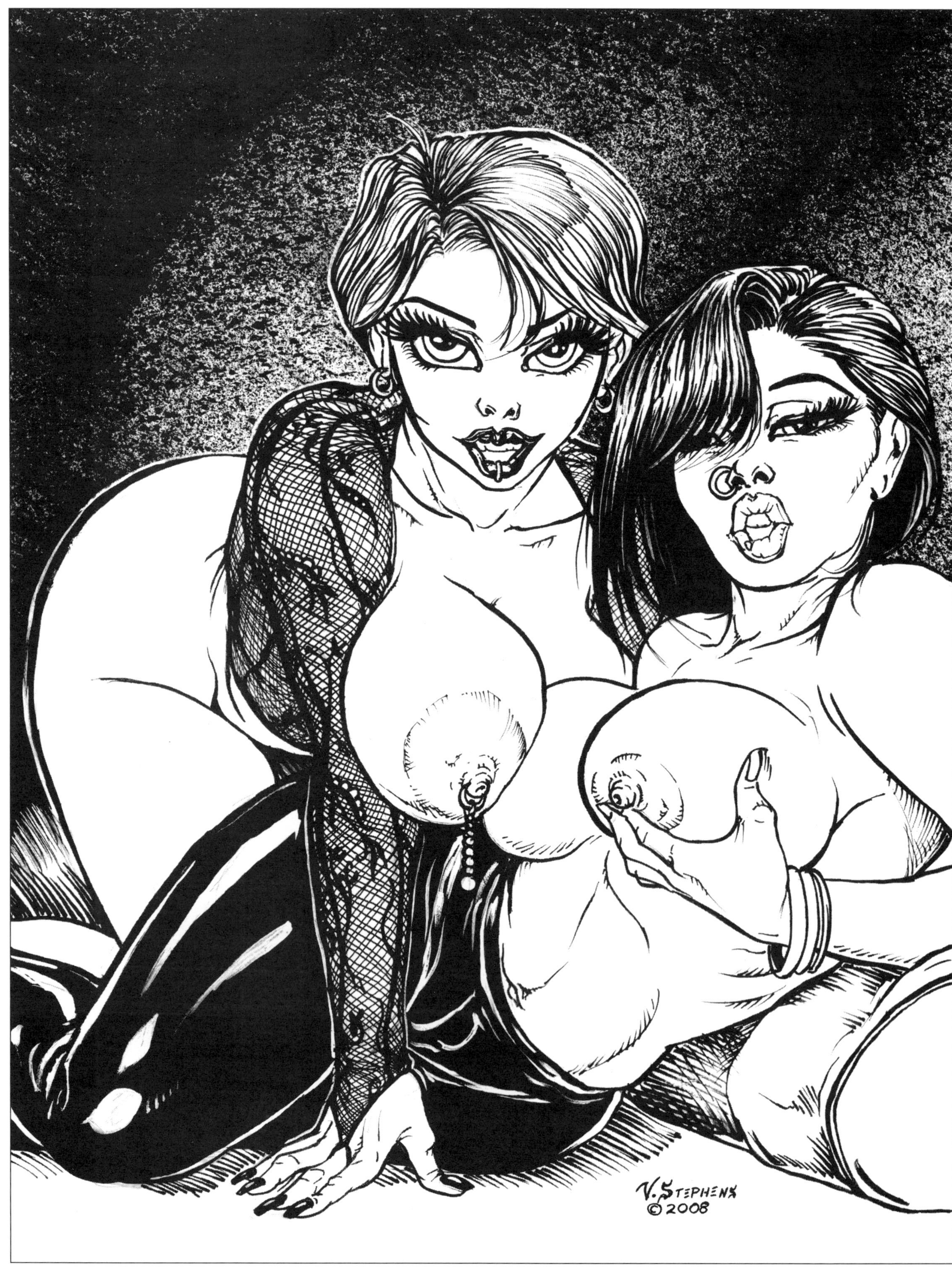
V. STEPHENS
©2008

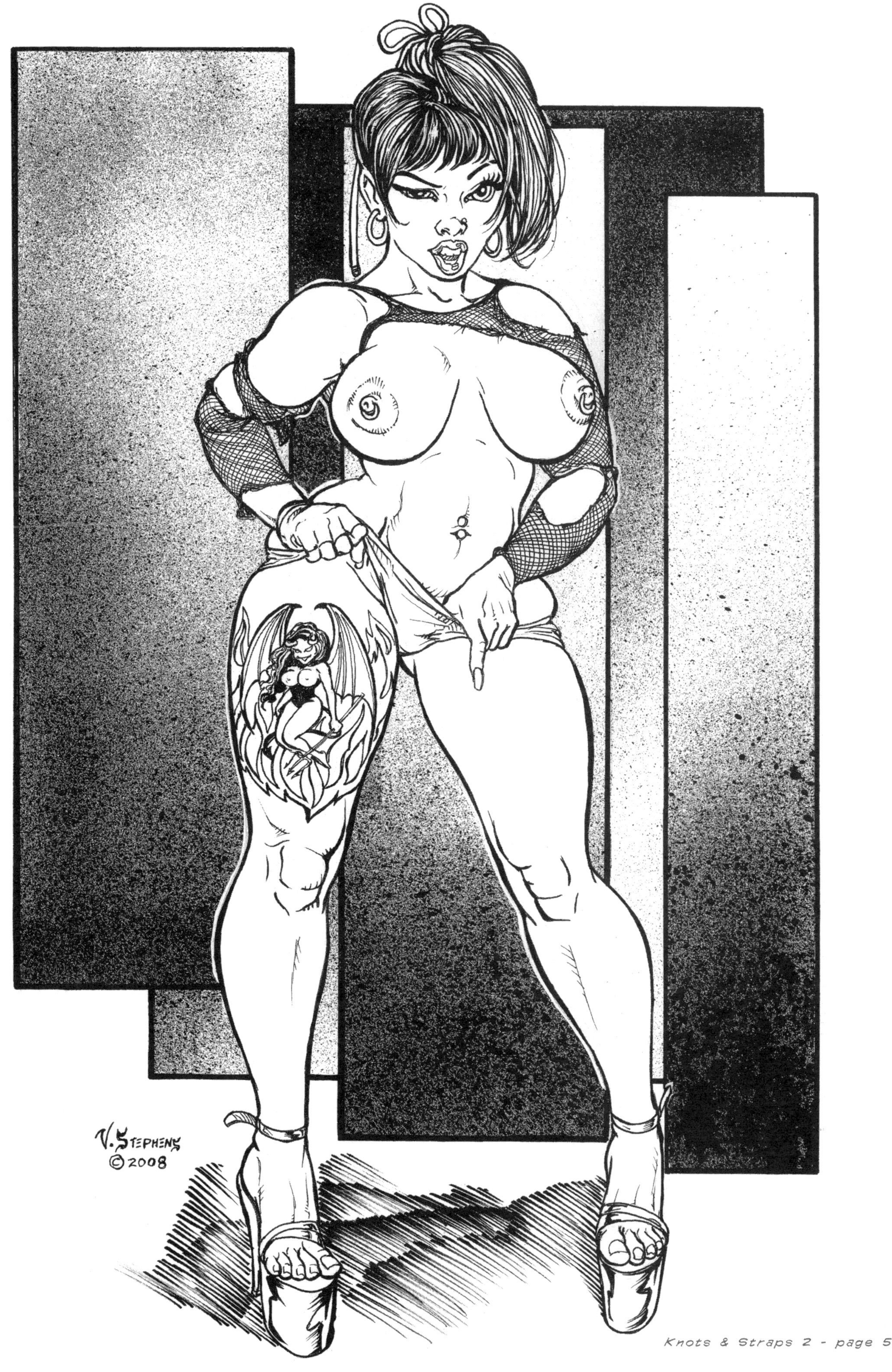
V. Stephens
©2008

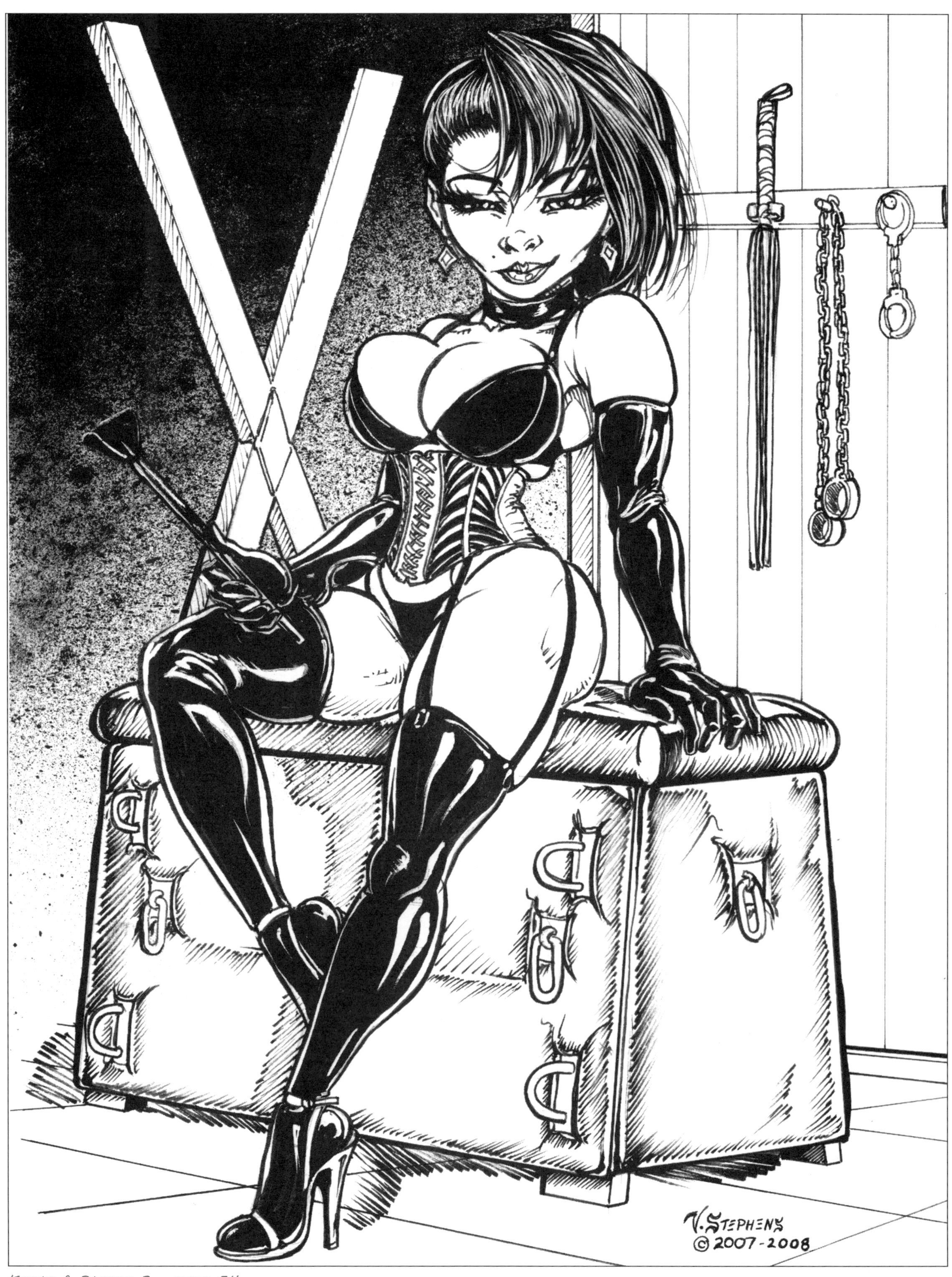
V. STEPHENS
© 2007-2008

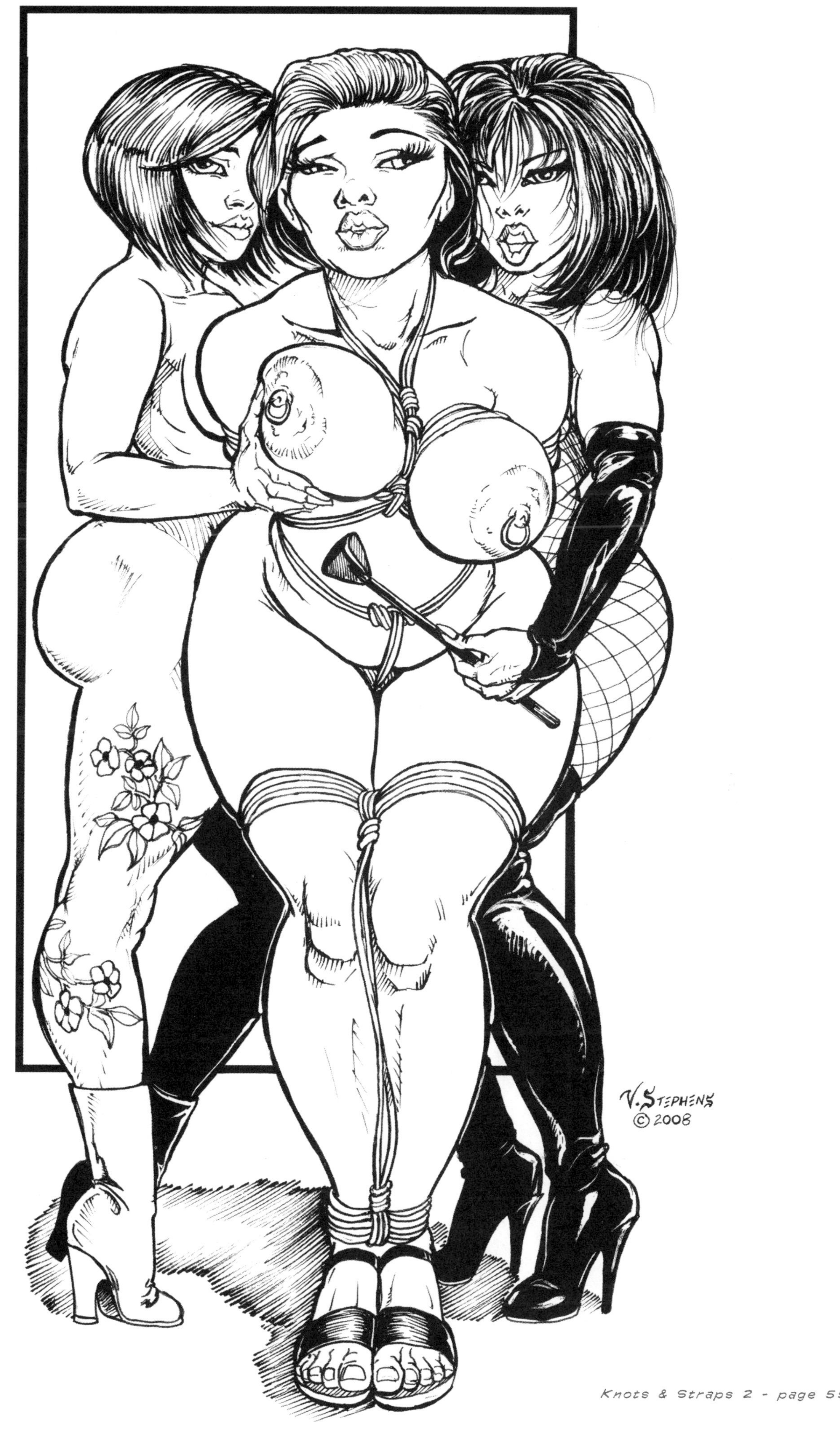
V. STEPHENS
© 2008

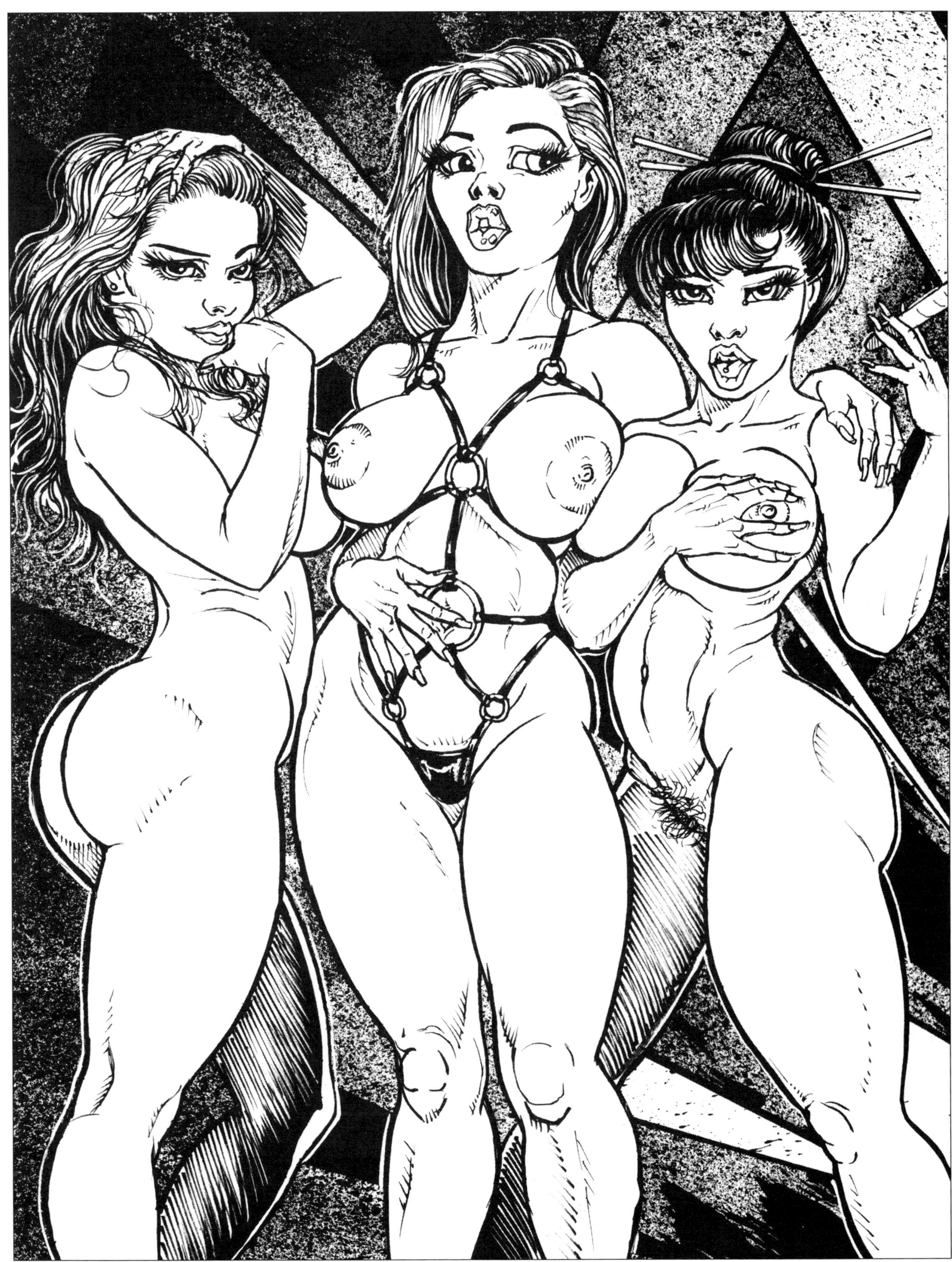

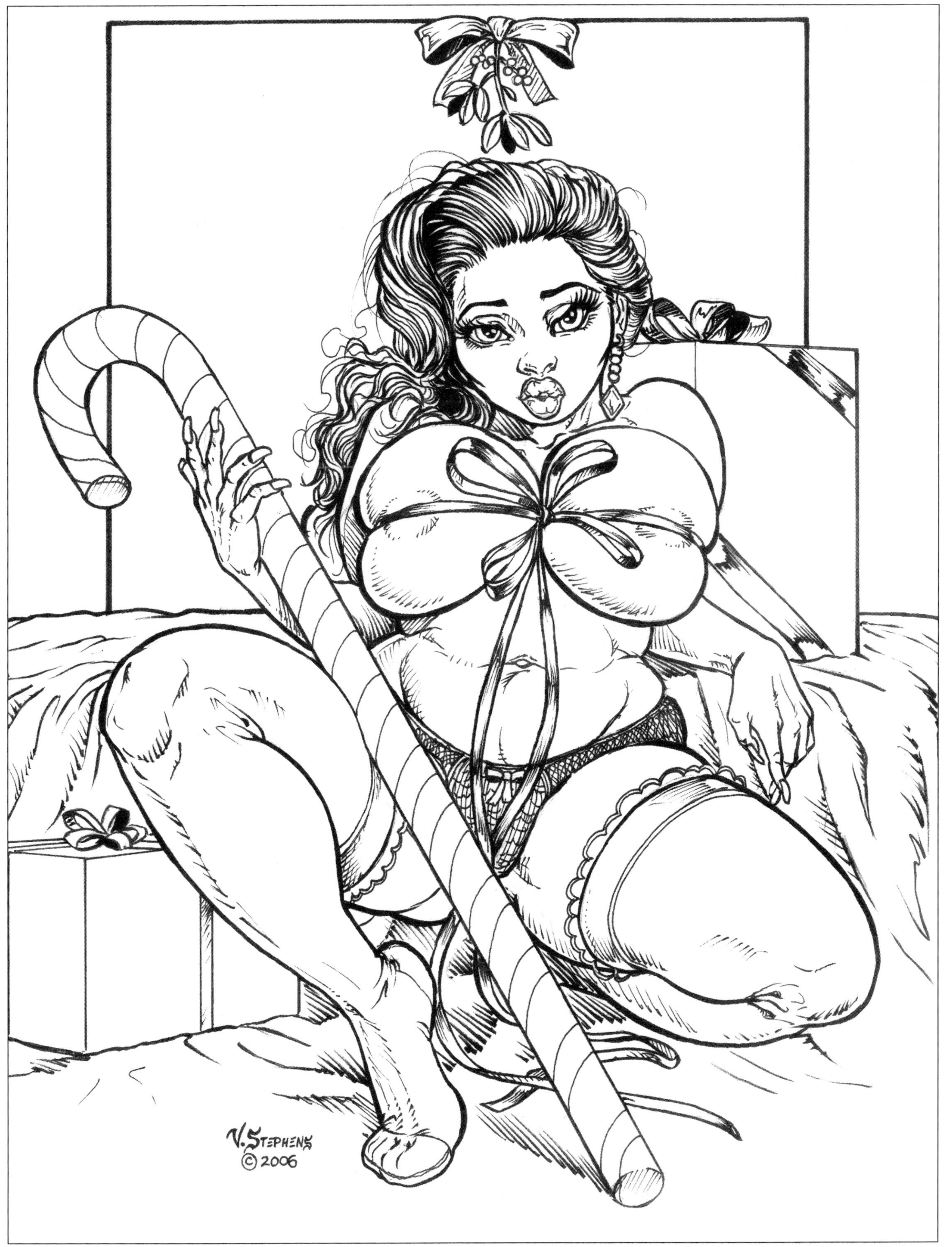
V. STEPHENS
© 2006

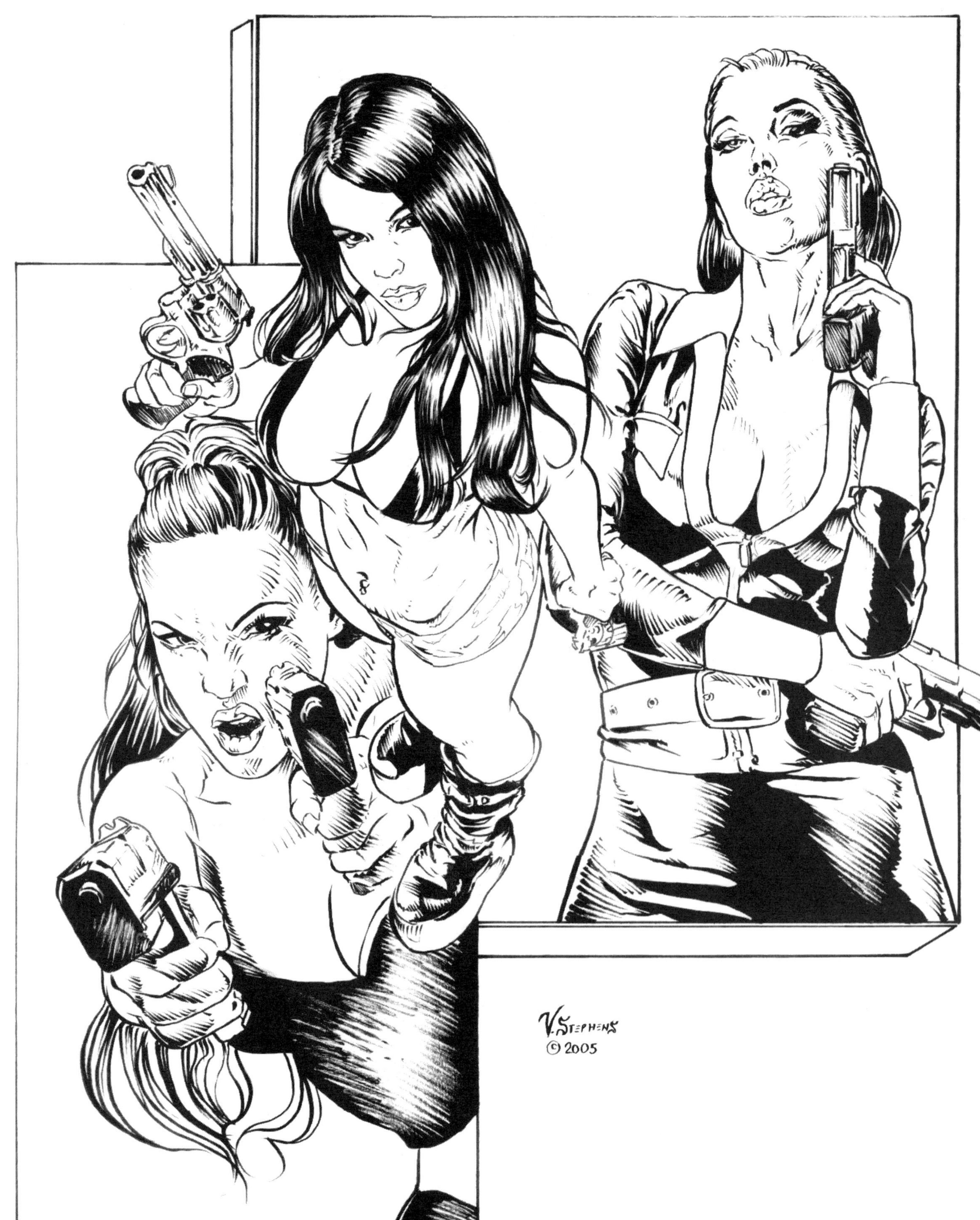
V. STEPHENS
© 2005

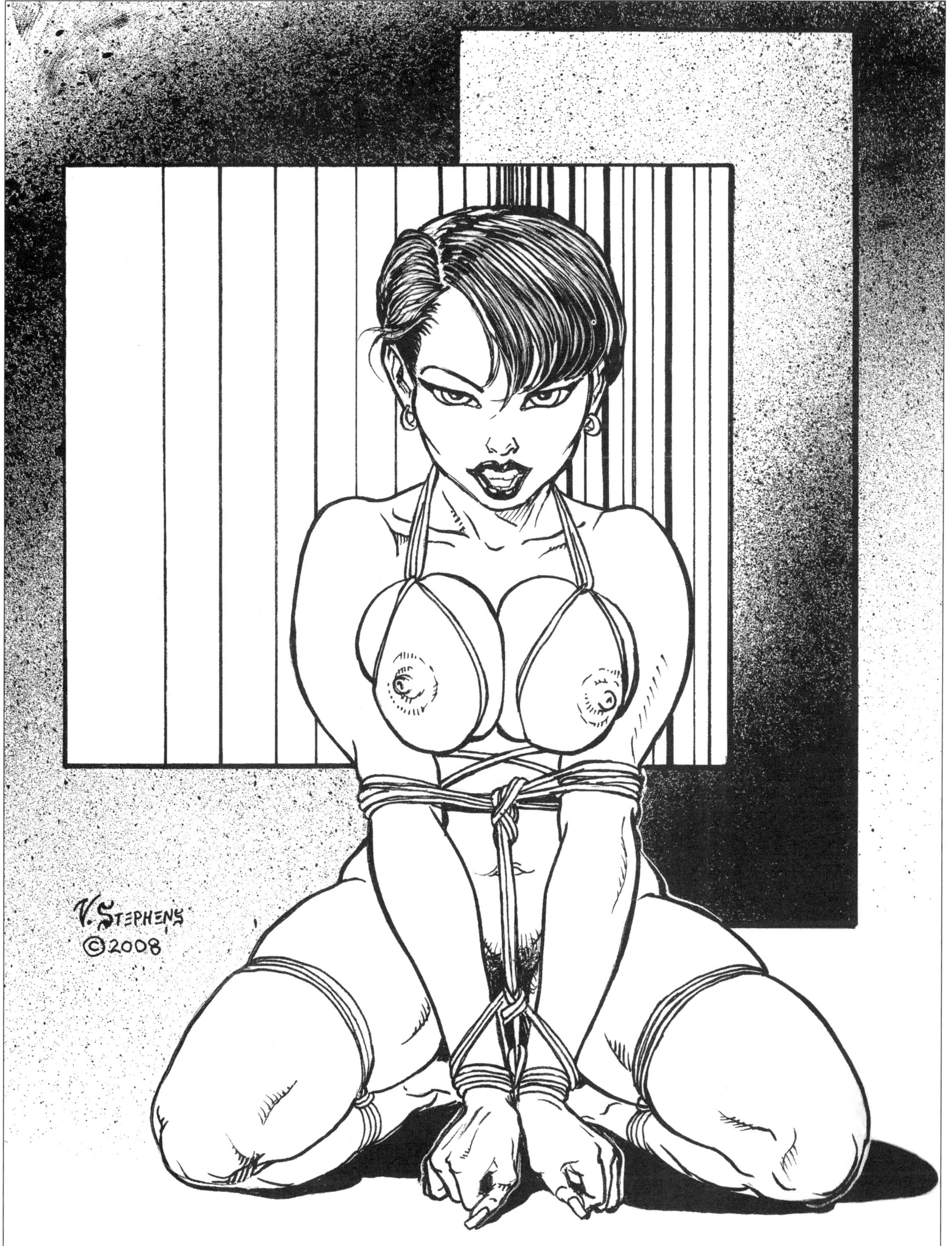
V. STEPHENS
©2008

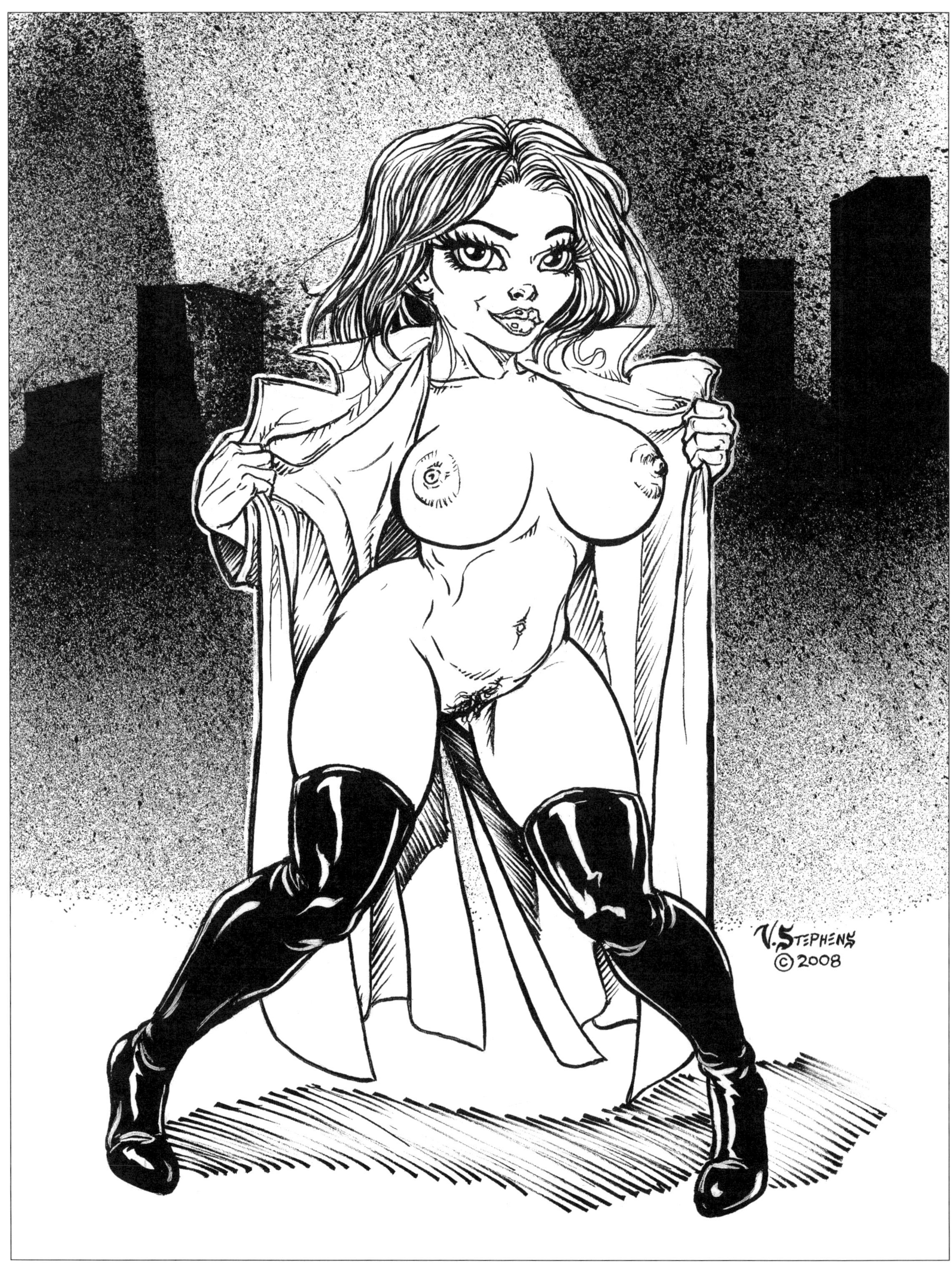
V. STEPHENS
©2008

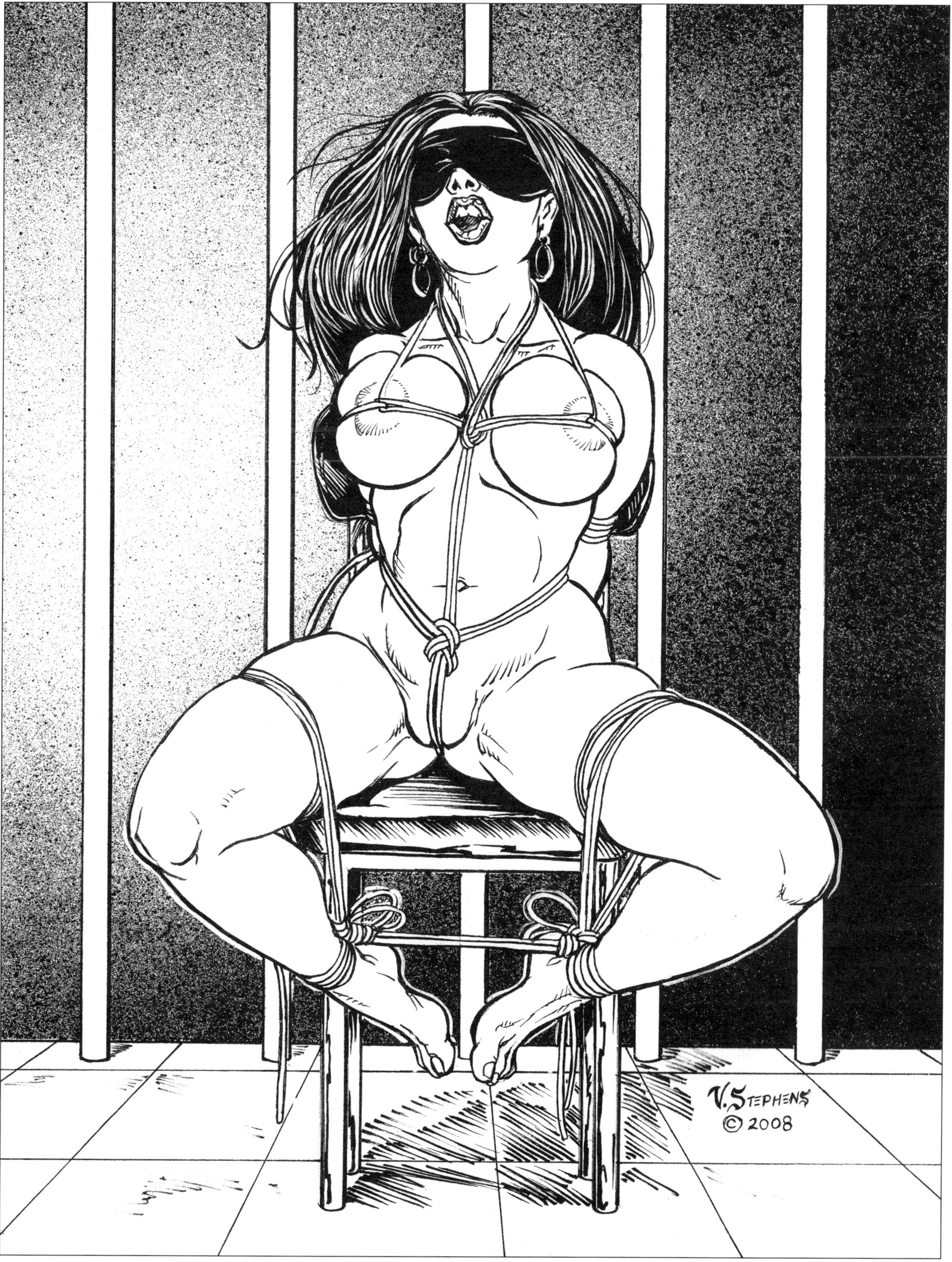
V. STEPHENS
© 2008

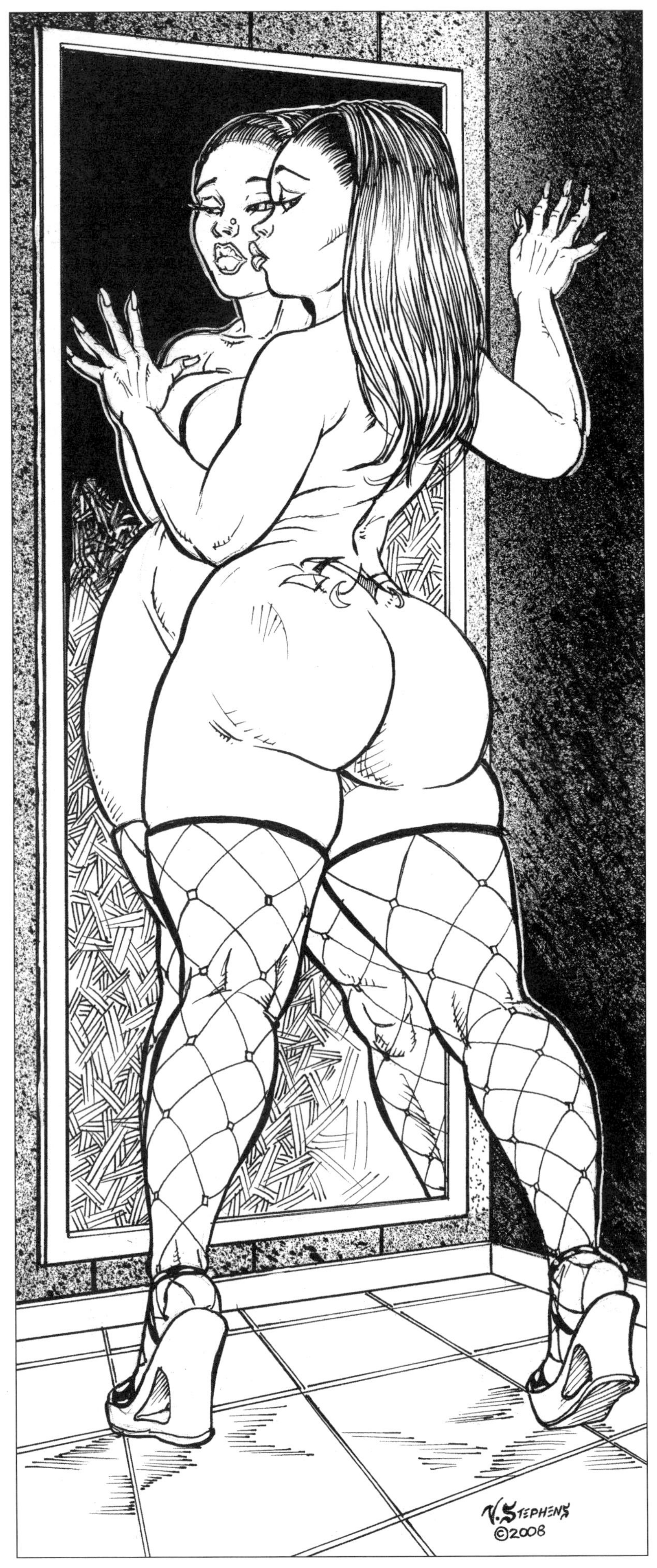
V. STEPHENS
©2008

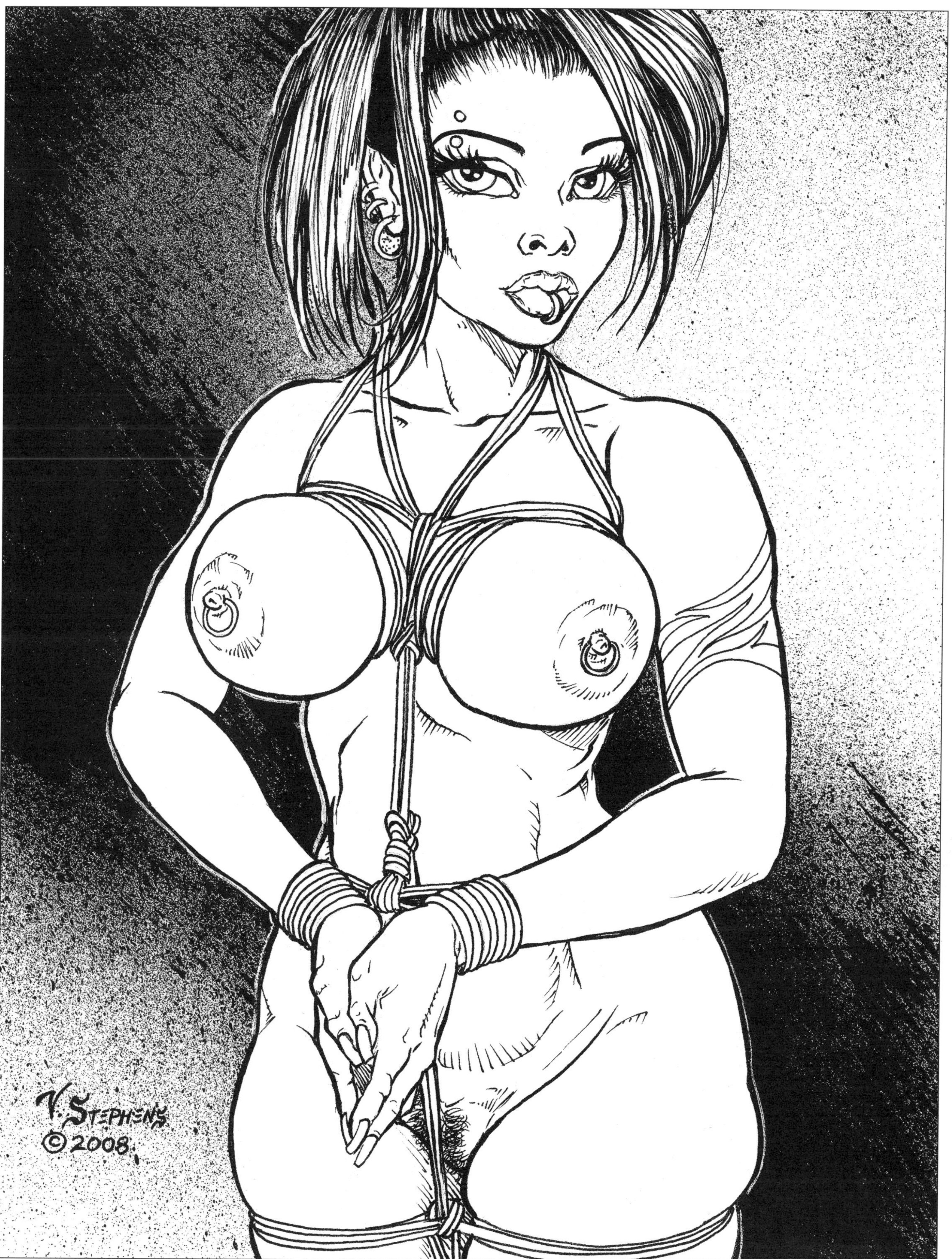
V. STEPHENS
©2008.

To be sure - Vincent Stephens will be back with another fine collection of luscious ladies. Until then, stay updated with his latest creations at:

www.ramstarart.com

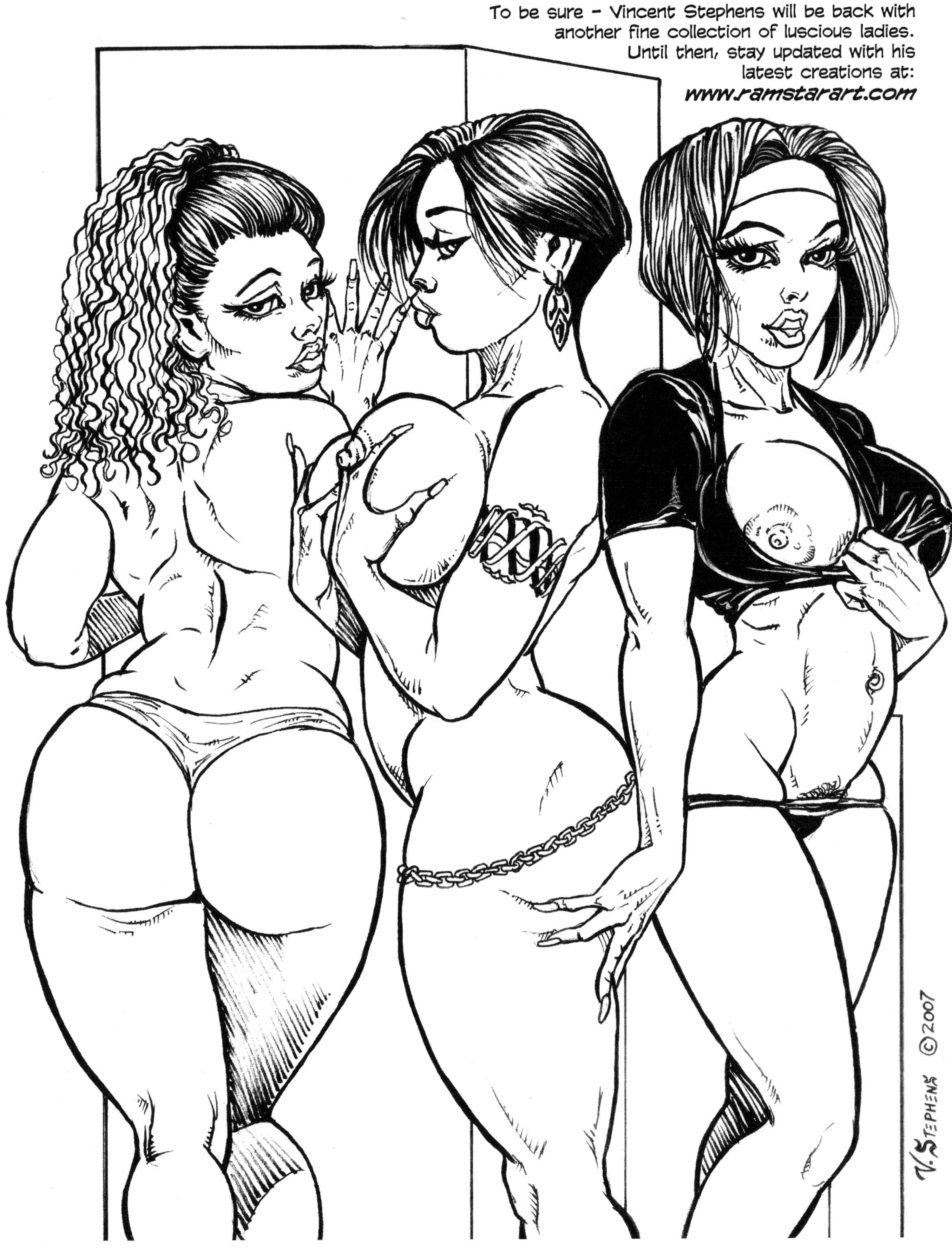